SECRET MONMOUTH

Louise Wyatt

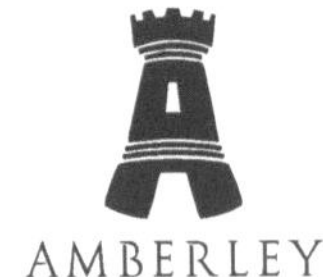

AMBERLEY

Acknowledgements

A special and grateful thanks to Mr Stephen Clarke MBE, FSA, MIFA, who helped with background information on the early history and supplied some amazing reconstructive pictures.

All images are my own, unless stated and shared by Creative Commons.

To Mark, with love

First published 2019

Amberley Publishing
The Hill, Stroud
Gloucestershire, GL5 4EP

www.amberley-books.com

ISBN 978 1 4456 8960 9 (print)
ISBN 978 1 4456 8961 6 (ebook)

British Library Cataloguing in Publication Data.
A catalogue record for this book is available from the
British Library.

Origination by Amberley Publishing.
Printed in Great Britain.

Appointed GPSR EU Representative: Easy Access
System Europe Oü, 16879218
Address: Mustamäe tee 50, 10621, Tallinn, Estonia
Contact Details: gpsr.requests@easproject.com, +358
40 500 3575

Contents

Introduction

Living not too far from Monmouth helped greatly while writing this book. Occasionally, I had passed through – or should I say, cut through – what I now know to be the suburb of Overmonnow and for me, like many others, Monmouth used to be a road sign off the busy A40 while traversing that road in the quickest way possible.

I'm glad that one day the decision was made to turn off the A40 to explore Monmouth once I discovered that the castle was the birthplace of Henry V. A few years and many trips later, I have attempted to put the more unknown history of the area and its environs into this book. What I discovered during researching was the amount of local people that have written about the area over many years, so I was very lucky to have lots of resource material coupled with more up-to-date discoveries. One of the better moments of research was meeting local archaeologist Stephen Clarke and seeing 5,000-year-old timbers!

Monmouth is a gem. There is so much history, so much archaeology tracing the area and its habitation from Neolithic and tribal peoples through to Romans and then the Normans. What I found both disappointing yet enthralling was the Battle of Monmouth in 1233. I had vaguely heard of it but only because I had visited the castle remains a few years ago and had a browse on Google. However, researching it for this book, I was both shocked and fascinated at how important it was, how bloody it was and how fearsome the rebellion was. It's hard to believe now, standing in a picturesque corner of South Wales, among visible history and romantic castle remains, just how much death and destruction happened here; that Monmouth had played host to the powerful barons and magnates of the day, as well as royalty. It's a shame the Battle of Monmouth isn't known more in mainstream history.

Monmouth became the county town of Monmouthshire after the Laws of Wales Act 1535 created five new areas, one being Monmouthshire, along the areas of the old Marcher lands, but it had been a corporate body since the times of Henry III, who granted Monmouth a seal and limited privileges in the mid-thirteenth century. It prospered from its market, which, according to Keith Kissack's book *Monmouth: The Making of a County Town*, was already established by the end of the eleventh century. The market was originally held in the outer bailey of Monmouth Castle, which in time developed into Agincourt Square.

It was also very difficult not to digress into the history of Monmouth's glorious buildings and monuments, many of which are listed. There is a plethora of writing and information regarding all of these but when researching – many buildings having so much to say – I had to curb my enthusiasm. Just as I did with the Nelson trip to Monmouth; it is well documented already but after reading about his travels in the Forest of Dean and to settle a dispute with the timber merchants in Chepstow, it would have been very easy to digress. If Nelson history is of interest, I can thoroughly recommend the Nelson display in Monmouth museum.

MONMOUTH, the county town of Monmouthshire, is a municipal and parliamentary borough, a market town and head of a petty sessional division, poor law union, and county court district, 128 Miles from London by road and 145 by railway, 31 from Gloucester, 16 from Abergavenny, 19 from Hereford, 10 south-west from Ross, 16 north from Chepstow, 55 from Bristol, 25 north-east from Newport, 35 north-east from Cardiff and 80 from Swansea; it is in the Southern division of the county, hundred of Skenfrith, rural deanery and archdeaconry of Monmouth and diocese of Llandaff. (Kelly's Directory, 1901)

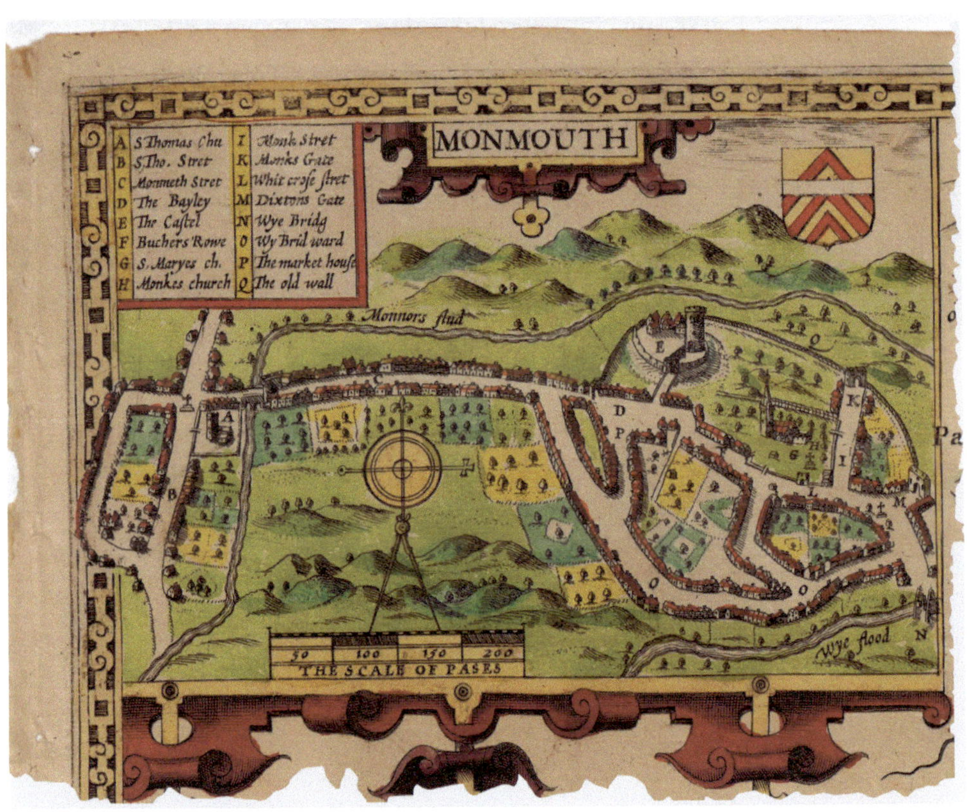

John Speed's 1610 map of Monmouth.

1. The Lost Lake

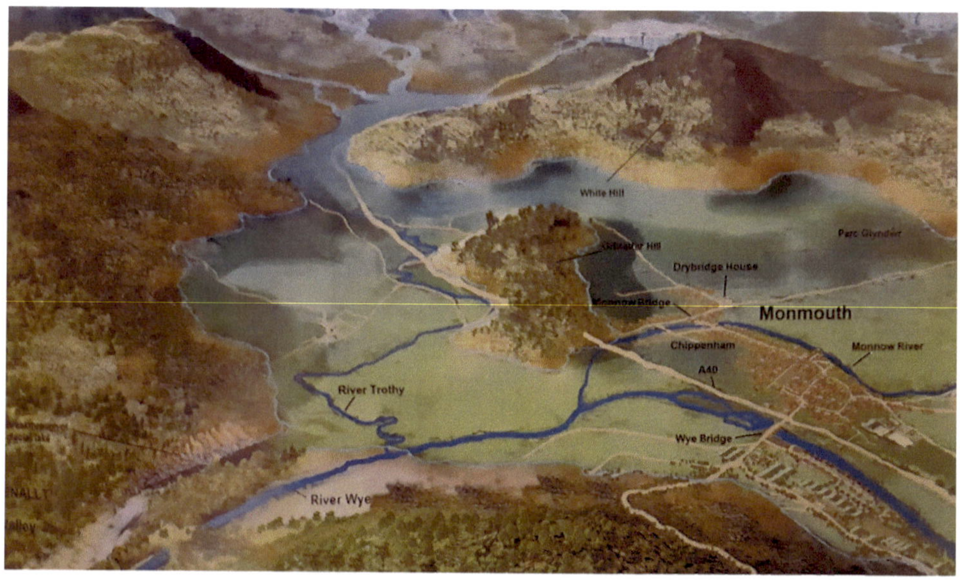

What the prehistoric lake would have looked like with modern-day landmarks to help with familiarity. Debris in the gorge between Redbrook and Monmouth created a very large (bigger than any lake in Wales today) post-glacial lake filling the 'Monmouth Basin'. (Image reproduced by kind permission of Stephen Clarke)

It is hard to believe that if one stands in Monnow Street today, looking towards the medieval bridge gate over the River Monnow, that not only are you standing on an ancient trackway and old Roman road, but going back further in time, you would have been standing underwater in one of the deepest and largest prehistoric lakes at the time. Part of the shore line would have been in the area of upper Monnow Street and St James Street; St James Square itself sits on a Mesolithic hunter-gatherer camp. Ancient remains of harpoons found in the area show peoples that lived and fished on the shore of Monmouth Lake, similar to the images below.

DID YOU KNOW?
At the highest spring tide around 2000 BC, the River Wye would have been approximately 10 metres above the level it attains now.

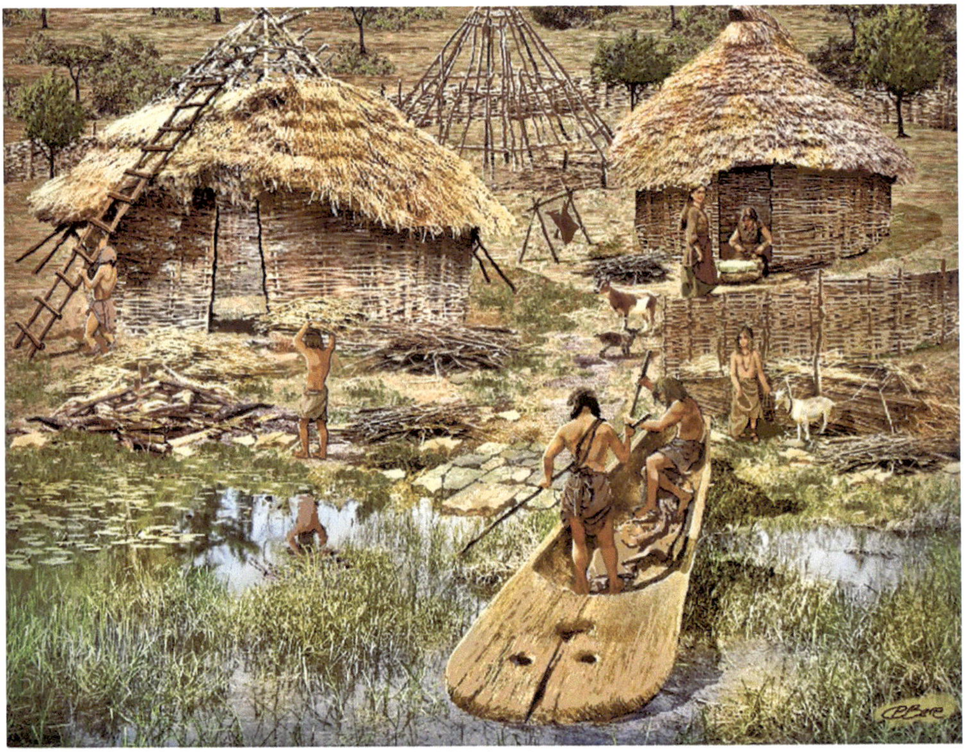

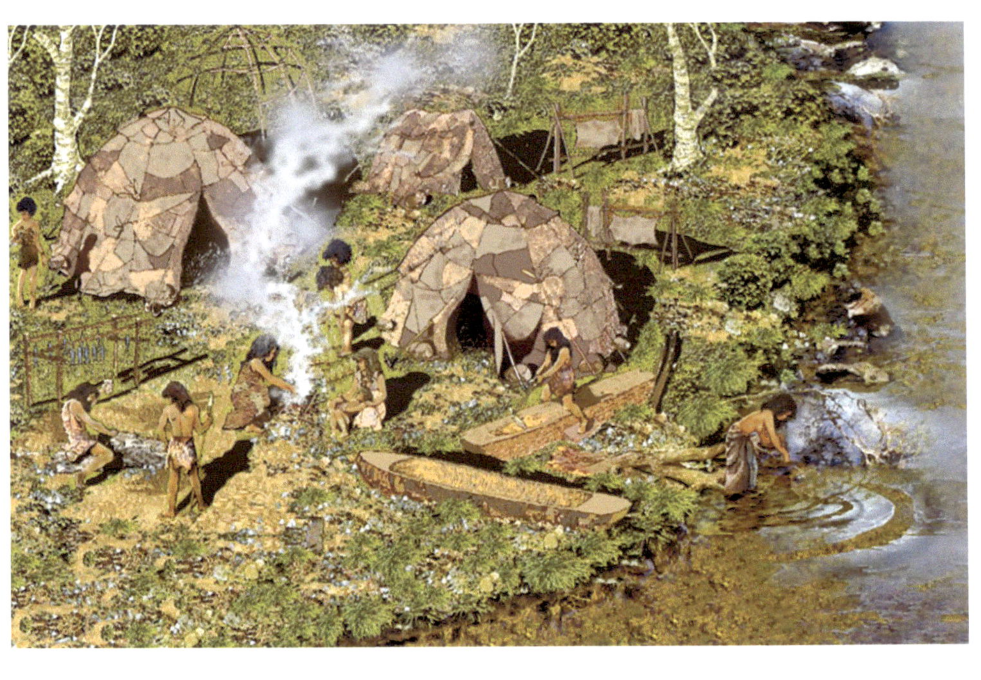

Above and below: Peter Bere's reconstruction of the Middle Stone Age hunter-gatherers' camp beside the lake. (Images reproduced by kind permission of Stephen Clarke)

Monmouth and its environs are rich in archaeology with valuable evidence making it possible to date and reconstruct the timeline and events that shaped this small corner of south-east Wales. After digging at a site of proposed housing estate at Parc Glyndŵr, archaeological finds soon unearthed a picture of Monmouth before the Romans came: the Great Lake, settlements, boatbuilding and the amazing find of timbers of a log boat, radiocarbon dated to around 3200 BC. Also, on the same site and radiocarbon dated to around 2920 BC, are what appears to be remains of a crannog, a house on stilts on a lake. While found in Ireland and Scotland, the only other known lakeside settlement in England and Wales is at Llangorse Lake, Brecon. The Monmouth crannog predates this one by approximately 2,000 years.

The archaeological record at Parc Glyndŵr shows that the shores of the vast lake, where it was joined by the busy River Monnow, had attracted human settlement for many thousands of years – from the Stone Ages through the Bronze Age and into the Iron Age; in fact, the only period when occupation was apparently sparse was during Roman times when the Monnow had taken its present course and little was left of the post-glacial lake or of its lagoon. (Stephen Clarke, *The Lost Lake*)

The lost lake of Monmouth eventually drained over millenia and remarkably was still evident as a lagoon until shortly before the Romans came.

DID YOU KNOW?
The dating of the timbers on the prehistoric lake show that they are 300 years older than the pyramids.

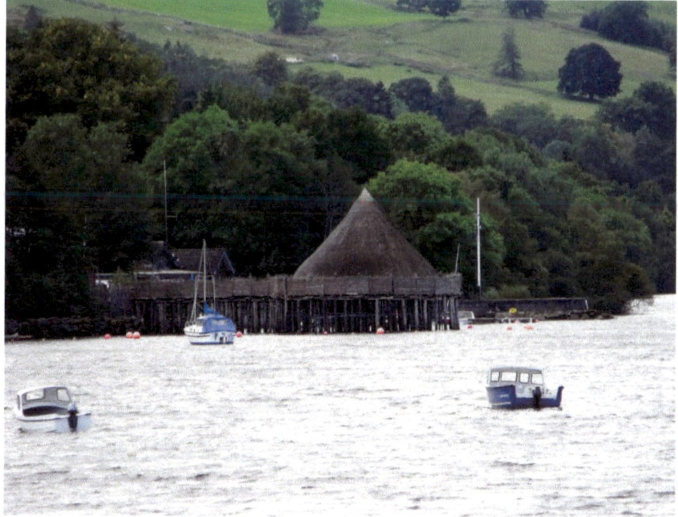

Example of a crannog. (Image courtesy of Nick MacNeill under Creative Commons 2.0)

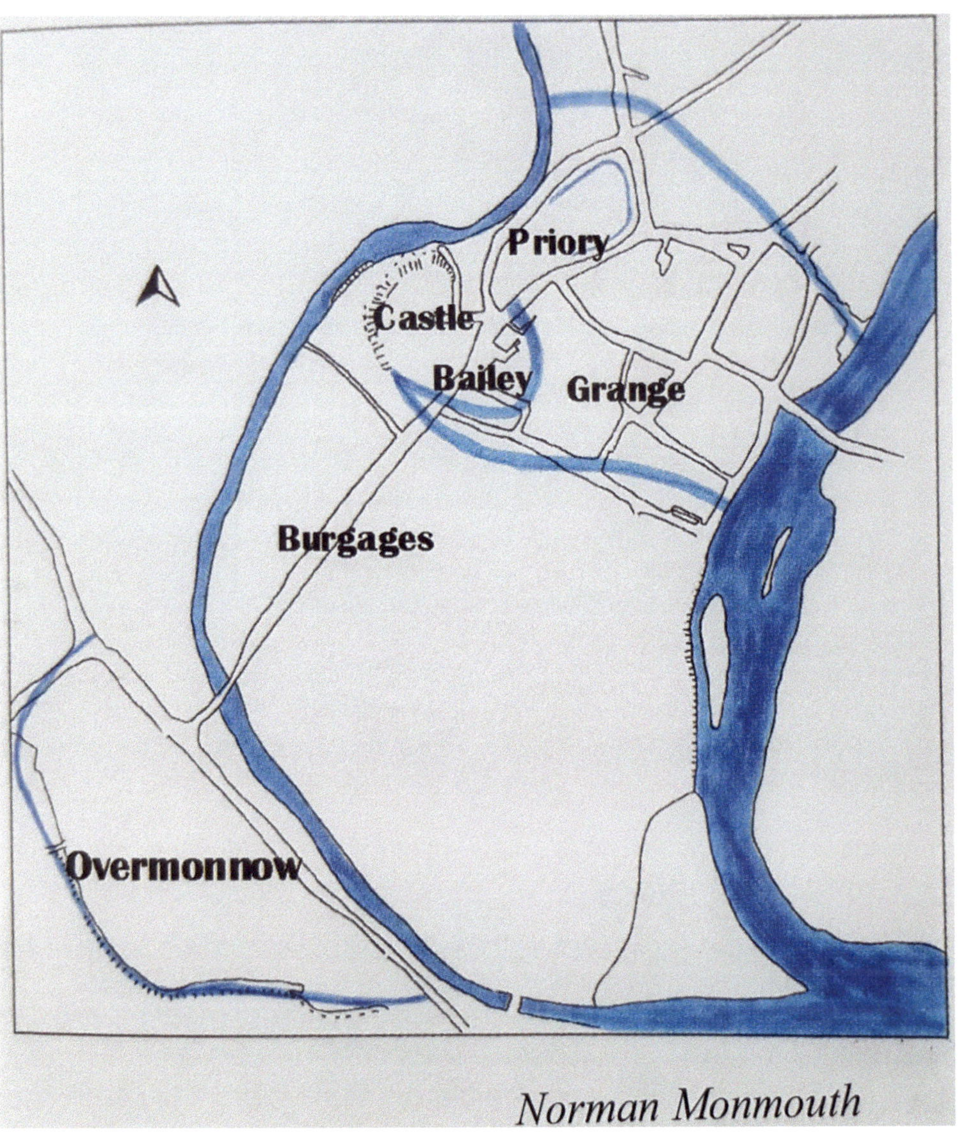

(Image reproduced by kind permission of Stephen Clarke)

2. Rivers and Roads

The River Wye is a paradox; an industrial waterway and an area of outstanding beauty do not usually go hand in hand. The beauty of the Wye has been the subject of paintings, poems, books and diaries since the eighteenth century. It holds the endearment of being the birth of the tourist trade since the river cruise known as the Wye Tour came into being:

> The Wye Tour (popular between 1782–1850) became extremely popular during the Napoleonic Wars (1803–15) when the customary European Grand Tour of the wealthy was not an option. The Wye Tour was inadvertently started by a wealthy rector in 1745 who took some guests on a boat trip from the rectory at Ross-on-Wye; thus began the Wye cruise, with sights such as Symonds Yat, Goodrich Castle and Tintern Abbey. In 1782, the Revd William Gilpin, whose readership included King George III, published his writings *Observations on the River Wye* ... and this made the Wye Tour ever popular. Chepstow was the final destination of the Wye Tour and there would have been a pier at the port area for passengers to disembark and make their own way back to their homes.
> *Secret Chepstow* (Wyatt, 2018)

The poet Coleridge (1772–1834) notes of the Wye: 'Oh what a godly scene ... the whole world seemed imaged in its vast circumference.' Wordsworth, while in the Tintern area, wrote: 'The waters ... rolling from their mountain springs with a sweet inland murmur.'

However, the Wye had also been an important industrial communication artery and Monmouth once had its own thriving quay, now the home of Monmouth rowing club.

Settlement along the River Wye is evidenced by the remains of hill forts using the river as a boundary on one side, including Symonds Yat, Little Doward, Piercefield at St Arvans and Bulwark at Chepstow. According to CADW, Welsh borderland hill forts seem to appear in phases around 500–400 BC.

DID YOU KNOW?
The River Wye shares its source with the River Severn from Plynlimon (meaning five peaks in Welsh) from the Cambrian Mountains. The Wye is the fifth longest river in Britain.

Iron Age people would have lived in small farming communities and the tribe around Monmouth (and south-east Wales) were called the Silures, who managed to hold off the invading Romans for around twenty years:

Above and below: Steps down to the River Wye where the quay used to be. Note the old mooring ring in wall.

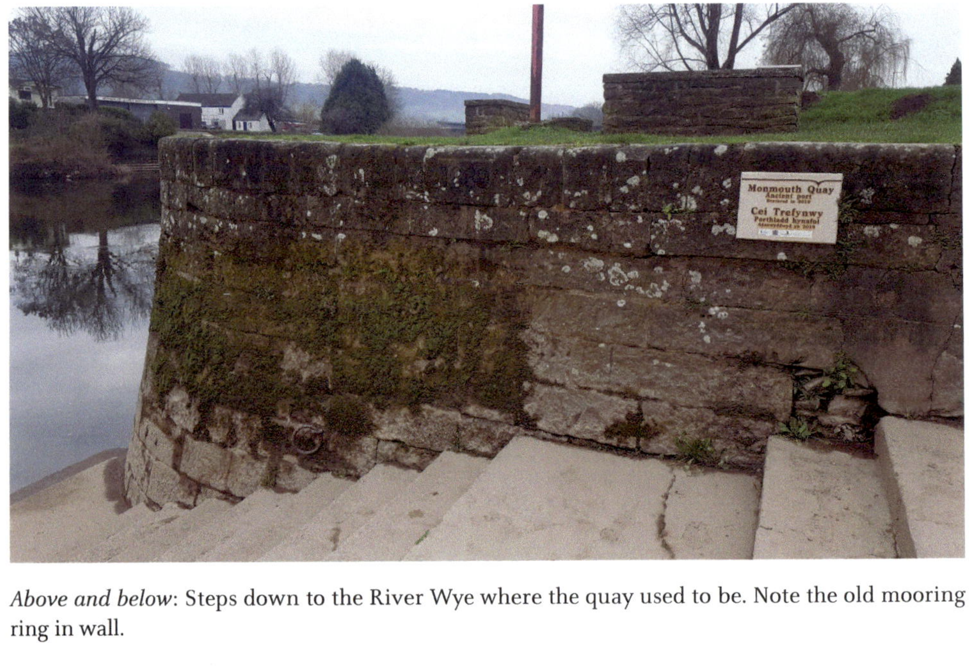

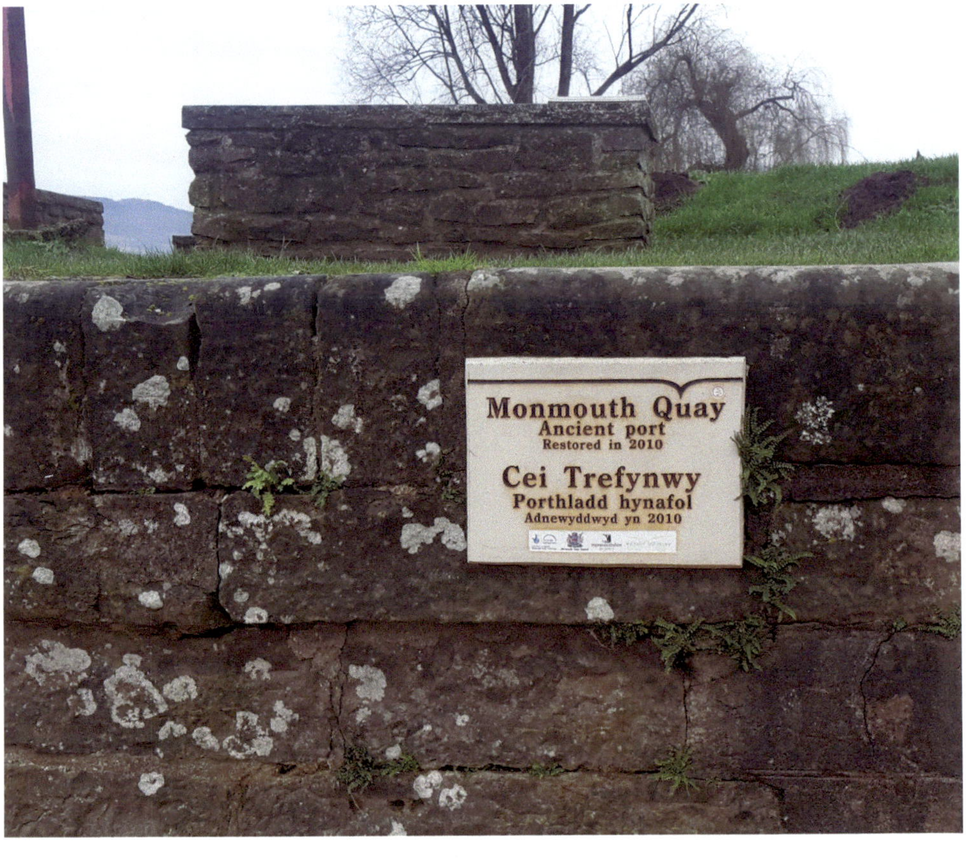

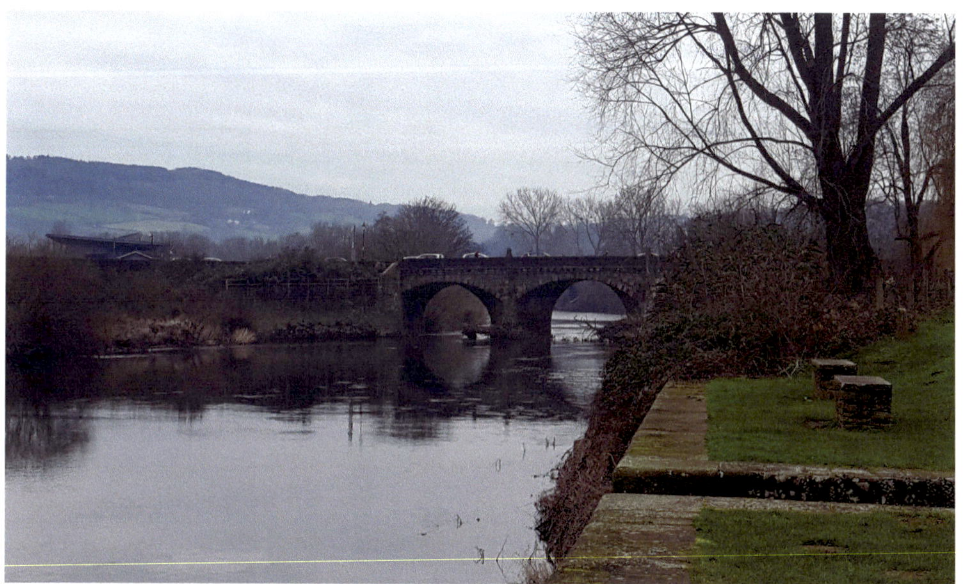

Looking downstream in the direction of Chepstow from the old quay towards the Wye Bridge, known as Monmouth Bridge in 1282 when it formed part of the Forest of Dean boundary. It would have originally been a wooden construction and now carries the A466, the turnpike road built in 1828 and completed in 1829, and follows the Wye Valley from just south of Hereford to Chepstow via Monmouth and Tintern.

The Silures were known to be a very fierce tribe and successfully resisted Roman conquest, including defeating what was probably the Twentieth Legion, in AD 52. Tacitus, the Roman Historian who chronicled the invasion stated:

'Conspicuous above all in stubborn resistance were the Silures. A naturally fierce people and now full of confidence ... every warrior bound himself by his national oath not to shrink from weapons or wounds. Such enthusiasm confounded the Roman general. The river too in his face, the rampart they had added to it, the frowning hilltops, the stern resistance and masses of fighting men everywhere apparent, daunted him. Ostorius, worn out by the burden of his anxieties, died, to the joy of the enemy.' Tacitus: Annals Book 12 [30] (www.sacred-texts.com).

The Silures were eventually subdued in AD 75 by the Roman General Agricola, Tacitus' father-in-law. According to John Davies in his *History of Wales*, the Romans believed a city was the key to leading a civilised life, so the Silures were granted a *civitas* (a social body of citizens who form a state) and Caerwent was born. The Roman name, *Venta Silurum* means 'market town of the Silures' and is partially carried through in the Welsh version, Caer-went, meaning 'fortified placed with a market'. The medieval kingdom place-name of Gwent is derived from Caerwent. *Secret Chepstow* (Wyatt, 2018)

Industry really flourished along the Wye from around the sixteenth century onwards and the stretch of the river from Monmouth downstream to Chepstow has many relics of past industries along its banks, including paper and watermills, iron forges, copper works and

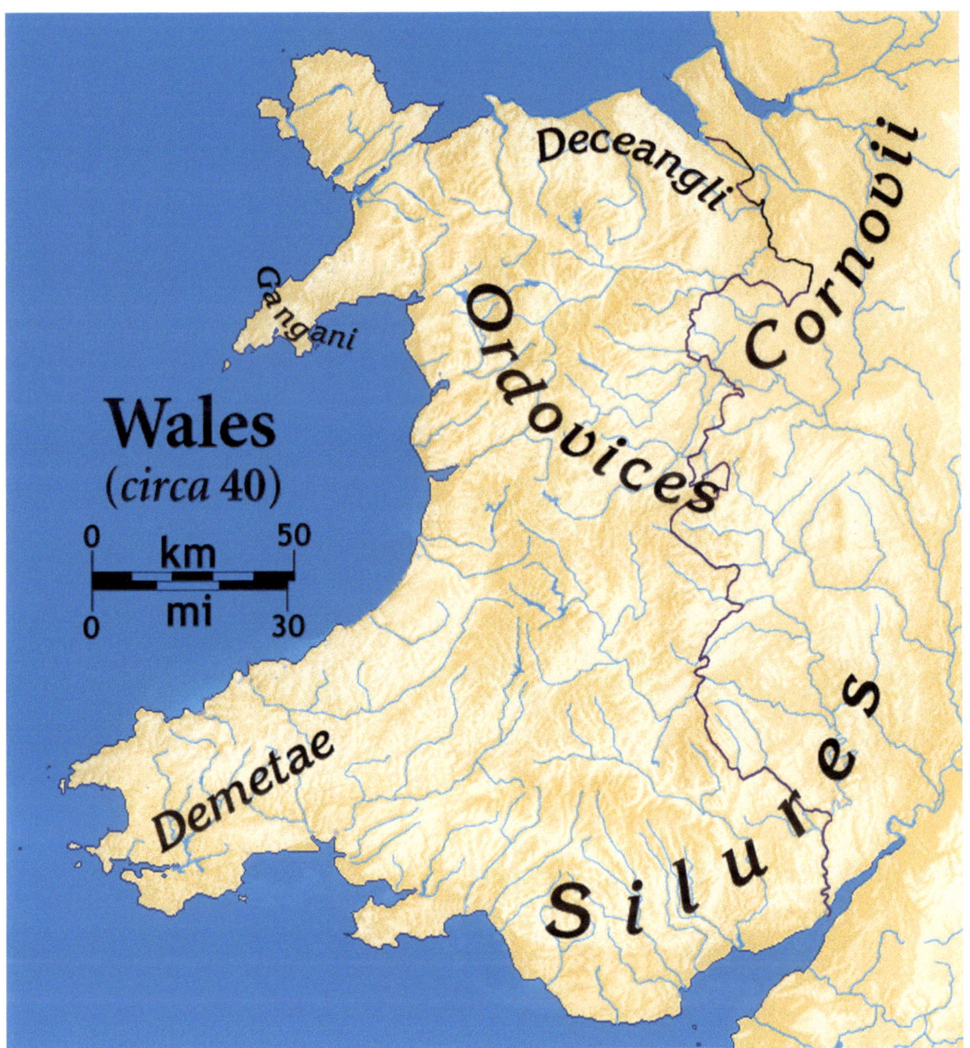

Wales at the time of the Roman invasion with modern Wales–English border for reference. (Creative Commons 3.0)

quays. The Wye can be likened to an artery, leaving the heart of its Welsh mountain source and carrying trade along its way to the important Severn Estuary, the watery gateway to Gloucester on the River Severn, Bristol a short distance across the channel, and beyond. Below is a snippet from the *County Observer & Monmouth Central Advertiser Abergavenny & Raglan Herald Usk & Pontypool Messenger & Chepstow Argus* (a rather long heading for a newspaper!), describing the route of the Wye from Hereford to Chepstow, with the stretch from Monmouth onwards described as 'a delightful aspect', dated 8 May 1869. However, on 24 October 1893, *The Evening Express* reports on the forming of a committee to report upon pollution on the Wye, with members being from Gloucester Council and Monmouthshire Council. Thankfully, the tranquillity of the Wye has survived more or less intact to modern day.

ts surface
and she
ared she
ed in the
she heard
contents,
ch being
d.   She
was only
l adhered
took to a
pper test,
ic.   She
r mother,
prisoner
re called,
evidence

RE.—On
ed in the
held near
l scarcely
d but few
re.   The
nt project
ing were
he British
emigrate

Bredwardine, which village stands upon an easy ascent, and appears in a happy point of view from the bridge. The stream passes along a rich and fertile country to Moccas, the seat of the late Sir George Cornwalle, Bart., and from thence to the city of Hereford. On quitting Hereford, the Wye bends its course towards Ross. Six miles from Hereford it receives the Lug, one of the three principal rivers of this county, and passing Mordiford, reaches Ross, where its meandering course is most attractive from the Royal hotel. From Ross it passes Wilton Castle, which is situated on its margin, and about two miles further is Pencraig, from which is a magnificient view; on the left is Walford village, and about two miles further on a bold promontory on the right is Goodrich Castle, and at a few yards distance is Goodrich Court, the residence of the late Sir Samuel Rush Meyrick, whose armoury has been lately removed to the Kensington Museum. Here the Wye in an extensive sweep reaches Lydbrook, and the next object on the right is Courtfield, where Henry V, was nursed by the Countess of Salisbury. The Wye next passes English Bicknor, and winding round Symond's Vat reaches Monmouth. Its course from Monmouth to Chepstow is of the same delightful aspect, and passes Bigg's Weir, Llandogo, Brock Weir, Coedithel Weir, Tintern Abbey, and pursues its course between the high romantic rocks of Windcliff and the Bannagor crags. It flows at the base of the extensive woods of Piercefield and the ruins of Chepstow Castle. Passes under the handsome iron and tubular railway bridges at Chepstow, and empties itself into the Severn about two miles below the town

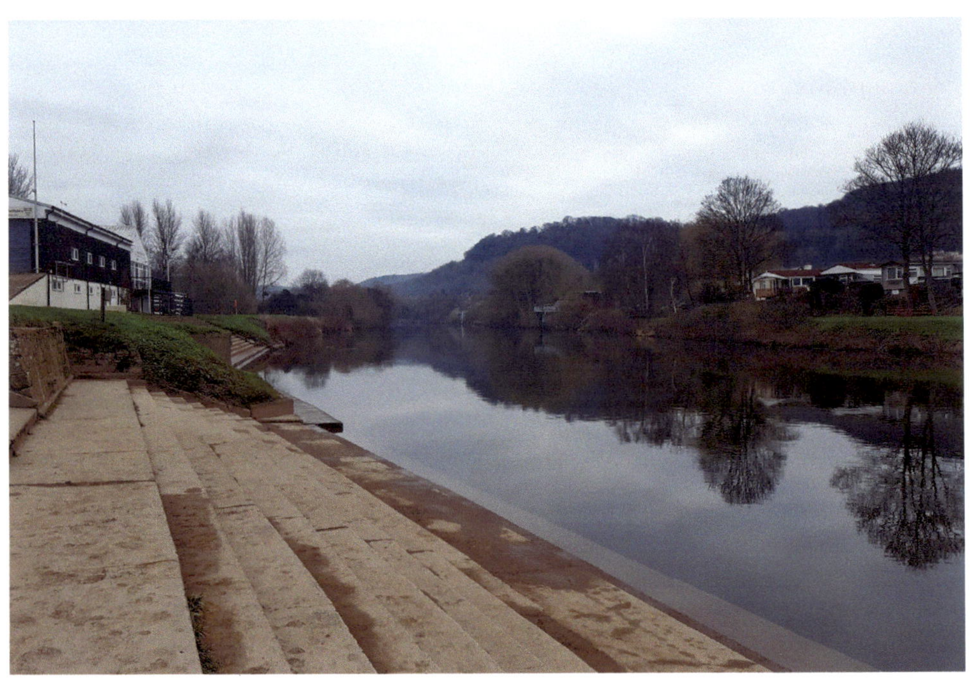

Looking upstream from the site of the old Monmouth Quay.

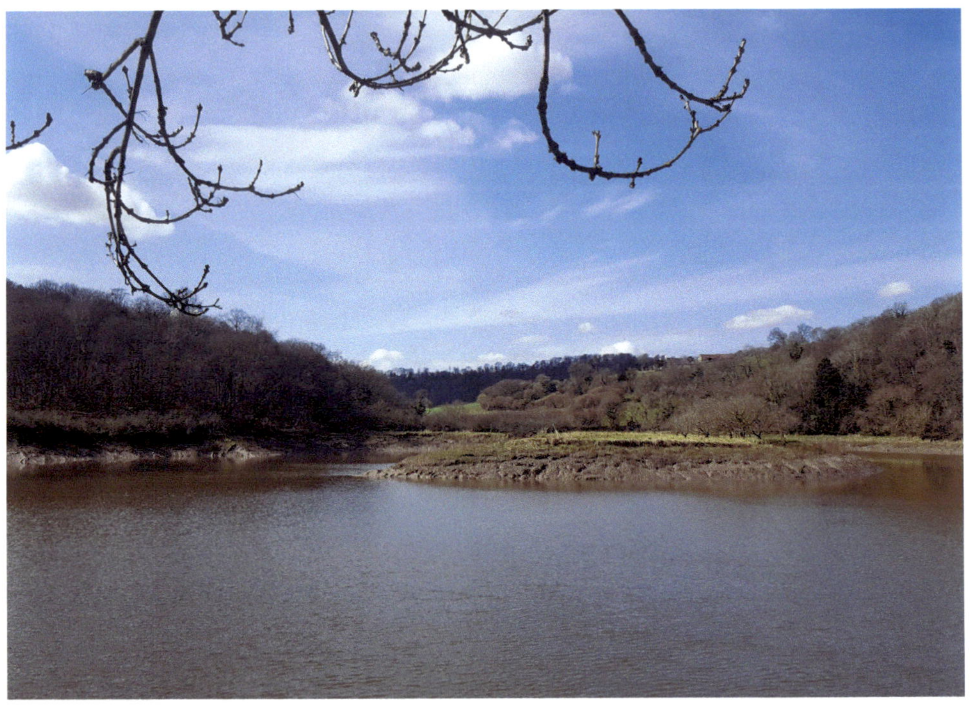

Looking from the deserted village of Lancaut on the River Wye, upstream towards Tintern and Monmouth. It is still picturesque today.

In 1801, *An Historical Tour in Monmouthshire* was published. This was written by the English historian and priest William Coxe (1748–1828) and includes a chapter entitled 'Navigation on the Wy'. A sign of the industrial artery that the Wye once was is highlighted in a paragraph from that chapter:

Brook's Weir, a village situated on the left bank, nearly halfway between Monmouth and Chepstow, exhibits the appearance of trade and activity. Numerous vessels from 80–90 tons where anchored near the shore, waiting for the tide, which usually flows no higher than this place. These vessels principally belong to Bristol and ascend the river for the purpose of receiving the commodities bought from Hereford to Monmouth, in the barges of the Wy, which on account of the shoals do not draw more than five or six inches of water.

In his book *Monmouth: the Making of a County Town*, Kissack notes that in the late eighteenth century, Coxe wrote Monmouth, as a town, was supported by neighbouring supplies trading with Hereford and Bristol via navigation of the Wye. The weirs on the river helped support over fifty mills and many industries with hydraulic water power but they also had a second use: fishing. However, issues between fishing and navigation brought problems with regards to the small water upwards from Monmouth to Hereford; trade with Hereford declined after 1800 due to the Wye upstream, but downstream to Chepstow, trade flourished with Bristol.

Just slightly downstream of the Wye Bridge, Monmouth once had a weir. Built in the Tudor period and standing at 11 feet high, it was dismantled in the late eighteenth century after many years of arguments at the disruption to navigation.

Rivers were really the way to the outside world and this is evidenced by the fact that the Wye valley road was not built until 1828. River trade in medieval times led to the prosperous growths of towns as very few areas were less than 15 miles from navigable waterways, while towns such as Ludlow and Winchester declined in importance due to being near unnavigable waterways. The significance of the Wye as a transport route was greatly reduced following the construction of the turnpike road through the valley in the nineteenth century; the Bigsweir Bridge was constructed as part of this turnpike road, which opened in 1829. The route of the turnpike road can be traced today along the line of the modern A466 road, which runs north through the valley, providing an easier means of communication than the river.

What road network, if any, was there while the river was the heartbeat of communication? We can see from the first chapter that human settlement had been around long before the Romans were here. Ancient roads were no more than trackways, usually linking local settlements and villages and occasionally a bigger route emerged to traverse the country where possible (such as the Ridgeway in Wiltshire – at approximately 5,000 years old, it is thought to be Britain's oldest road and was a trading route that connected Dorset to Norfolk). Until the Romans began the road network in Britain, the country was criss-crossed by these trackways and although finds from the continent have been found in British Iron Age graves, showing there was overseas trade, one can imagine how important rivers were for local communication.

Medieval roads were affected by variables such as pilgrim routes, church and corpse roads, monastic routes and drovers' roads. Royalty travelled extensively with their entourage and we know that King John visited Monmouth Castle (discussed in a later chapter). John Leland, the English poet and antiquary, travelled extensively in 1540 but made hardly any mention about the state of the roads. However, writing in 1586, William Harrison, the English clergyman who wrote 'Description of England' as part of The Holinshed Chronicles, remarked on the deterioration of highways. Two possible reasons for this given by Paul Hindle in his *Medieval Roads and Tracks*, is a) the Dissolution of the Monastries – the monasteries had been responsible for what little road maintenance there had been – and b) rapid growth of the Tudor economy equalling a sharp rise in trade and travelling, which the roads simply couldn't cope with.

DID YOU KNOW?
William Gilpin was responsible for bringing the word 'picturesque' into English culture via the aesthetics strand of philosophy. He first used it while writing his *Observations of the River Wye* in 1782.

Writing in 1873, Waugh notes in his *Illustrated Handbook to Monmouth* that:

Previous to the formation of our turnpike roads in 1755, and for sometimes afterwards, waggons were not in use in Monmouthshire; and grain and all other merchandise were conveyed on the backs of pack horses. When it is considered that all grain then sold in the markets was vended in bulk and not sold by samples, as at present, once can picture the busy and laborious scene which was wont to take place in this town on Saturdays.

Monmouth, a typical market town where the fortunes of the town depended on trade, had trouble with its surrounding roadways due to its geography, similar to Chepstow. Steep hills, clay soil and busy traders all added up and Kissack notes how the roads in and out of Monmouth were narrow and ran between steep banks. The Hereford road needed outriders to check and warn of oncoming waggons as if waggons met head on, then the waggon going downhill had to have its horses removed and dragged to a passing place. Kissack also notes how the Wonastow Road 'was little more than the bed of the stream which now runs beside it'.

In his *History of Wales*, Davis notes the appalling condition of Welsh roads and unlike in France, Britain's roads were not considered the responsibility of the government and only developed as per local demand, over the years ... In 1663, the first toll road opened – The Great North Road – and the first turnpike was erected on the Hertfordshire section. In his book *Turnpike Roads*, Geoffrey N. Wright states that this new concept of tolls – whereby the cost fell upon the traveller as opposed to the parish – took another thirty years to establish and the first turnpike act was introduced by 1700. Turnpike trusts were given powers to borrow money for managing roads and responsibility for repairs; there were a growing number of these trusts throughout the eighteenth century and tailing off during the nineteenth centuries, mainly due to the arrival of the railways. Between 1753 and 1839, over 200 turnpike trusts were authorised by parliament in Wales – these trusts were responsible for the upkeep of the roads but were also open to corruption and inefficiency. *Secret Chepstow* (Wyatt, 2018)

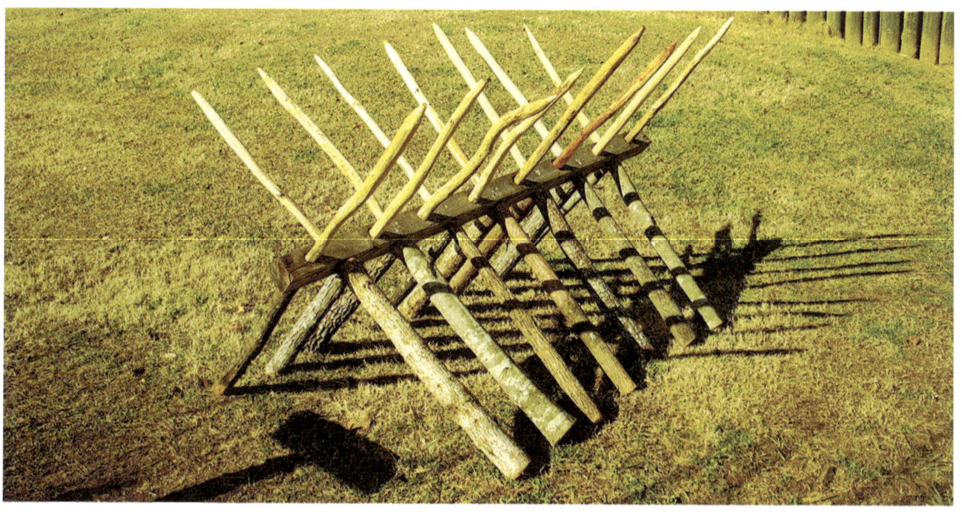

Chevaux-de-frise, a medieval anti-cavalry defence structure. Turnpike earned its name from the early design of the gates, similar to a *chevaux-de-frise*, and was quite literally a pike laid across the road until the toll was paid, whereby the pike was moved to allow one's journey to continue. (Image courtesy of Brian Stansberry under Creative Commons 3.0)

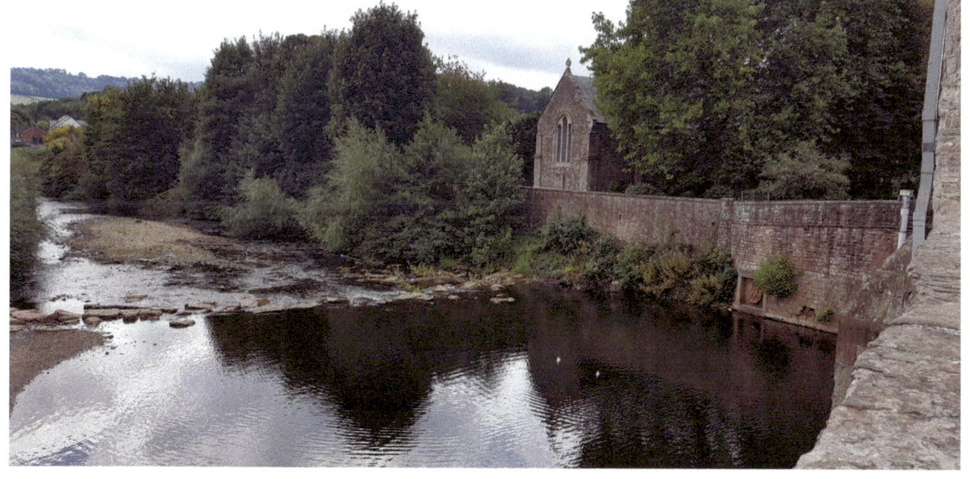

Looking at the small weir on the River Monnow from the Monnow Bridge.

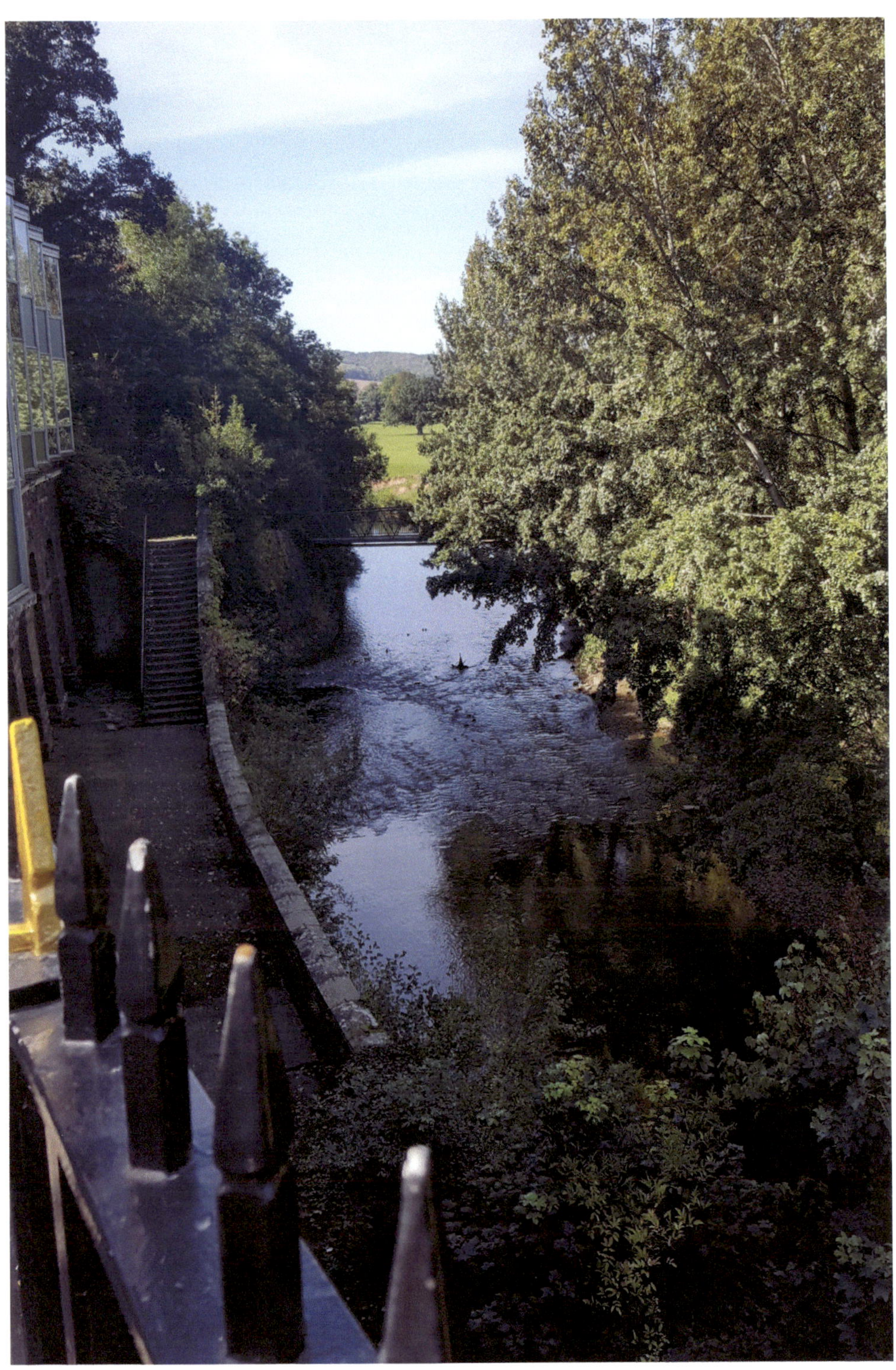

The River Monnow with Castle Field (Vauxhall Fields) in the background, most probable site of the Battle of Monmouth, 1233.

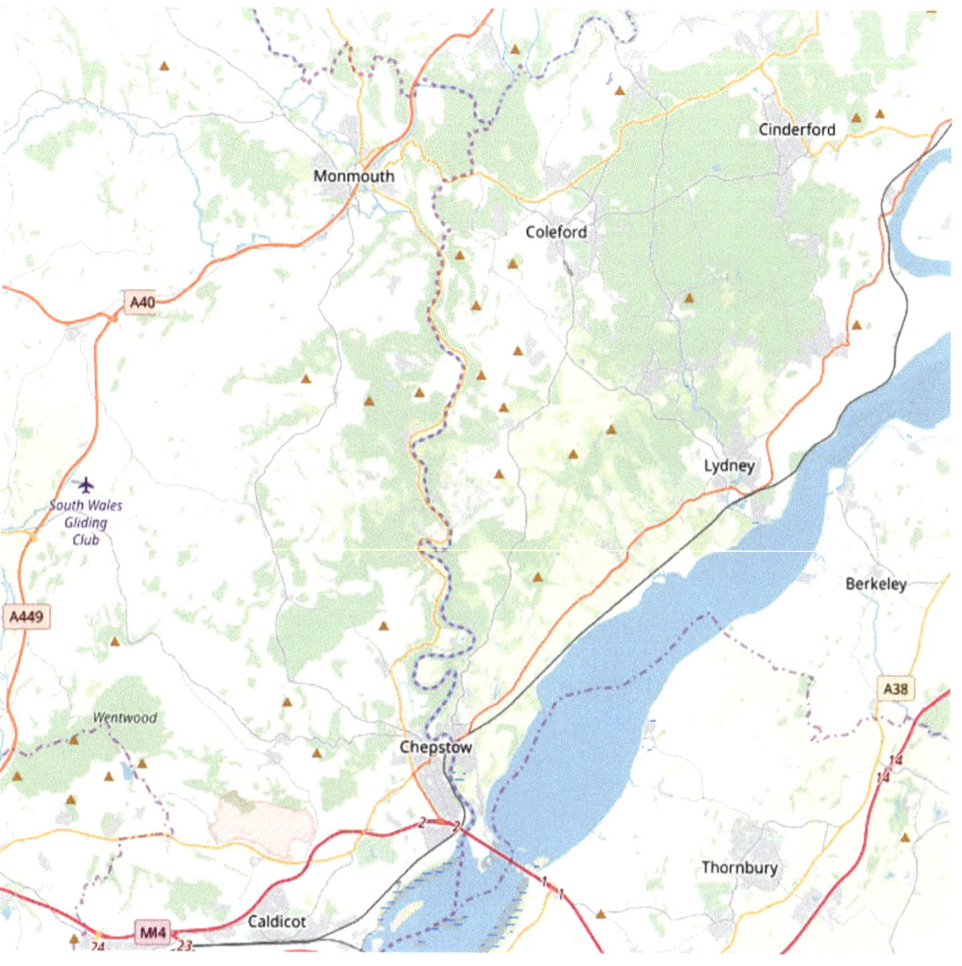

Map showing how the road (orange line) between Monmouth and Chepstow was built to follow the ancient waterway of the River Wye (blue dotted line). (Image courtesy of OpenStreetMap contributors under Open Database Licence)

The London to Oxford route, now known as the A40, crawls out of London town as the Western Avenue via Ealing and Uxbridge where it is then the M40 onto Oxford and back as the A40 onto Gloucester and thus into Wales. *Secret Hayes* (Wyatt, 2018)

The modern A40 follows the old Roman invasion and trade route that crossed over the Severn into Gloucester and the River Wye at Ross, the route passing across Monmouth and Westwards to Carmarthen and beyond. The most westerly Roman roads are to be found in Wales as, despite some evidence of mining and forts in Cornwall, no Roman roads have been found to date. Wales has a circuit of Roman roads with tracks criss-crossing the country, one of these may have been the Roman road out of Overmonnow.

When one crosses the Monnow Bridge leaving Monnow Street today, you walk out into the suburb of Overmonnow. In his book *Roman Roads in Britain,* Margary (1973) states that the Roman road from Monmouth to Usk may have followed an ancient route across the Monnow, out eastwards through Overmonnow and carrying the road westwards towards the village of Wonastow (roughly following the Wonastow Road) where there are remains of a Roman fort. The Roman road, Margary believed, carried on via Jingle Street to Dingestow, then to Raglan and onward to Usk. Margary based his findings on the Antoine Itinerary document, one of the very few documents that has survived by being copied from the original Roman era and providing details of names and clues to Roman sites, as well as their roadways. The Antoine Itinerary was possibly written over two centuries but nevertheless, it confirms there was a Roman road out of Monmouth.

This could possibly have been an ancient, pre-Roman route given the recent prehistoric findings and it is quite significant that the small medieval footbridge that crosses the *Clawdd-du*, or Black Dyke, is in direct line with Monnow Bridge and Monnow Street, a feature noted in the book *Monnow Bridge and Gate* by Rowlands, and possibly the sign of an ancient trackway. Flint tools and evidence of Bronze Age and Iron Age settlement have been found along this route in Monmouth and Overmonnow.

The prominent local archaeologist Stephen Clarke notes how this area and the ancient route through Monmouth and Overmonnow has attracted invaders and settlers for thousands of years.

CLAWTHY, OR CLAWDH-DHU.

[WELCH,—THE BLACK DITCH.]

Croffing the ftreet, and proceeding up the lane in front to a gate on the right hand, which we pafs,—in the courfe of a few yards we arrive at the ancient MOAT, bearing the above name, that formerly defended the Monnow Town. To the curious obferver, this moat is worthy of attention, as it ferves to confirm what has been advanced refpecting the very early fettlement of this part of the borough.

It forms a complete femicircle,—beginning at the Dry Bridge and extending to the Cinder Hill turnpike,—at each of which points it communicates with the river

Charles Heath, local printer and antiquarian, writing about Monmouth in 1804 and describing walking across the Monnow Bridge, crossing the street and straight ahead up a lane into Overmonnow (now housing).

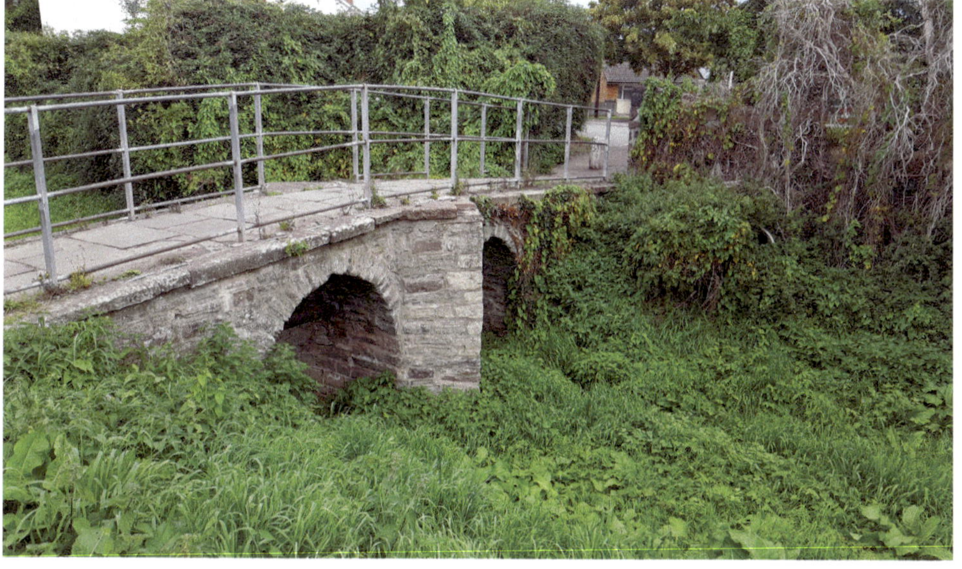

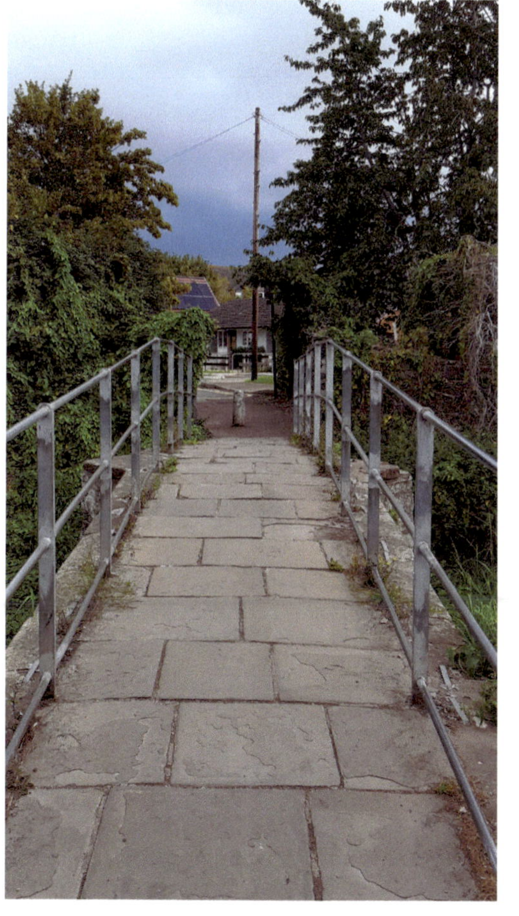

Above: The Grade II listed medieval bridge with unfortunate modern railings.

Left: Looking back across the medieval stone bridge over the Clawdd-du, back towards Monmouth town, this is in direct line with Monnow Street and Monnow Bridge in Monmouth and the route of an ancient roadway.

Part of the Clawdd-du or Black Ditch, which once had up to 40 feet of water and banks as high as 5 feet as a defence to protect the suburb of Overmonnow and defined the area until the 1930s. Now surrounded by modern housing, what's left is a Scheduled Ancient Monument.

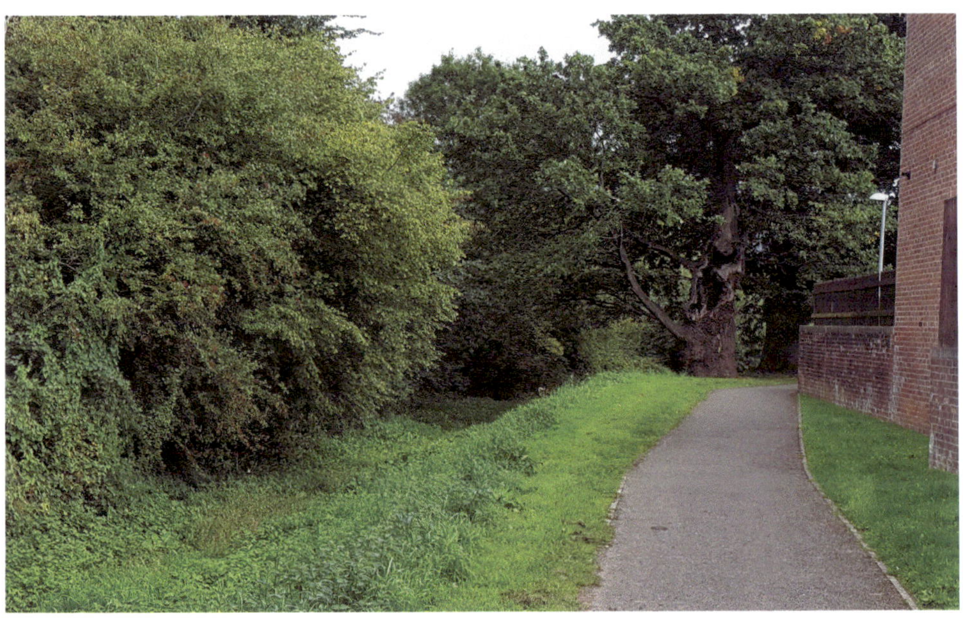

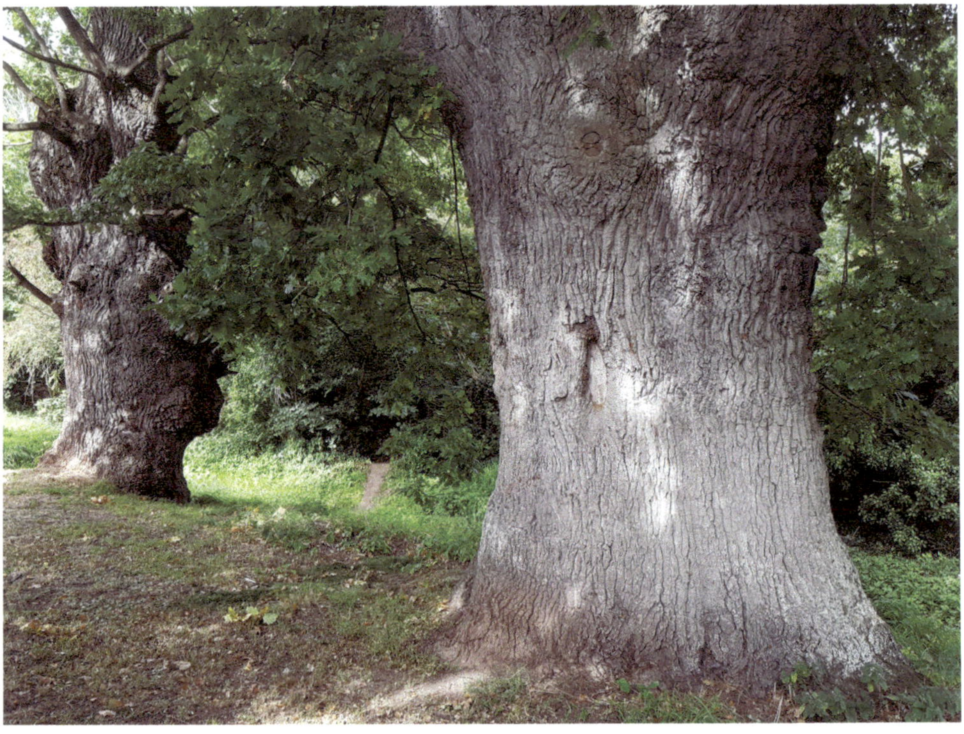

Ancient trees running alongside Clawdd-du.

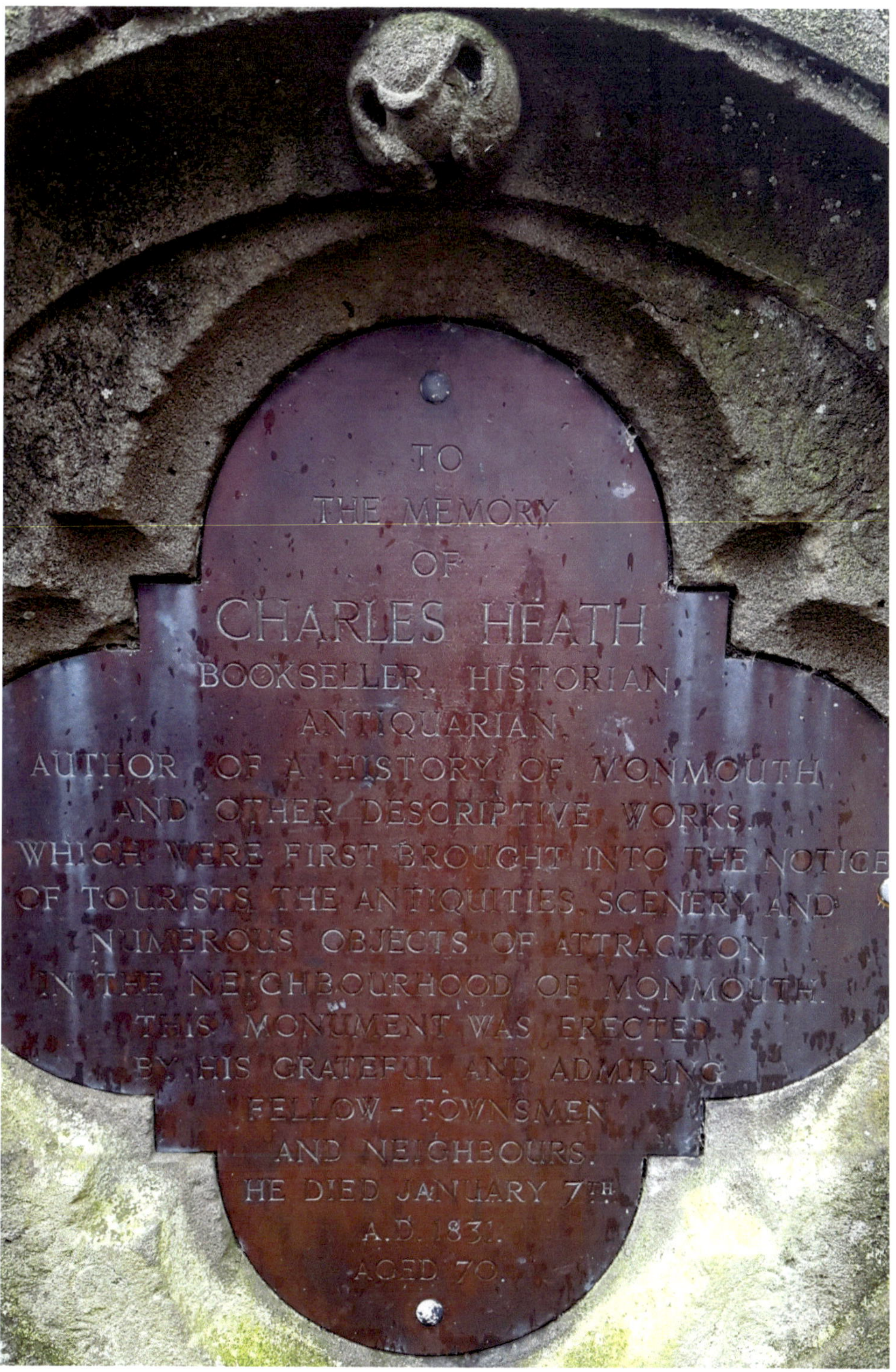

Grade II listed but quite difficult to read, the inscription on Charles Heath's memorial inside the gate of St Mary's Church.

3. Industry

We have seen in previous chapters how industry has been in this area since the Neolithic period. In the first century AD when the Romans invaded, they chose Monmouth as the site of a fort (which would be one of many along the Monnow Valley due to the fierce resistance they met against the Silures tribe, as mentioned earlier). The Monmouth fort, possibly built around AD 55, was on the main route to the fort at Usk, Wales' first legionary fortress, which was built around AD 54. There is nothing to see of these forts now as both are buried under the modern towns, although Monmouth's fort is marked by a blue plaque on Lloyds Bank, Monnow Street. This marks the exact spot according to the Antoine Itinerary as 11 Roman miles from Usk fort and 11 miles from a fort near Ross. A superb amount of archaeology also exists.

By the second century AD, the fort had become a settlement known as Blestium with an industry of iron working. Remains of forges have been excavated at Overmonnow and finds such as Samian pottery, Roman spearheads, walls, hearths, cremations, ditches and pits within Monmouth show how an important and viable site this was considered.

Iron forging continued to be a main industry in the area. However, Monmouth also had a flourishing market by the end of the eleventh century as burgesses paid low rents and were in possession of favourable building sites, probably due to the Laws of Breteuil that FitzOsbern had introduced to encourage settlers into a border land. According to Kissack, this helped the area grow into an important borough, helped by the pivotal castle and the wealthy priory. The fortunes of Monmouth Priory did fluctuate somewhat; in 1291/2 Pope Nicholas IV ordered both the temporal (physical) and spiritual finances of parishes in England, Ireland, Scotland and Wales to be assessed. A tenth of this revenue was to defray the cost of a crusade that King Edward I had sworn to undertake. This assessment was known as the Taxatio Ecclasiastica and remains an important source document to this day. At this time, Monmouth Priory was assessed at £86: £23 of temporal value and spiritual value of £63 and only third in rank of Benedictine wealth after Goldcliff and Brecon – nearby Chepstow was valued at only £35. The priory controlled 480 acres of arable land as well as drawing pensions from churches and property. However, a few years later the priory had fallen on hard times, due in part to bad management and a particularly nasty murder in 1309 (a local craftsman, John Carpenter, escaped prison, sought sanctuary in St Mary's but was dragged out by his enemies and murdered in the grounds; services could not be held there for a while).

DID YOU KNOW?
In 1545, John Falconer, a capper from Gloucester, left £40 in his will towards the rebuilding of Chepstow Bridge. That is the equivalent of approximate £25,000 today, showing cappers would be earning good money.

By the mid-thirteenth century, Henry III had endowed a seal and list of privileges giving Monmouth a corporate body from an early time. We know the market was a bustling centre of business and trade by around 1300 as Edward I had granted a murage (toll) in 1296/7 after the lord of Monmouth, Henry of Lancaster, had interceded with the king to levy a charge on imported goods into the town; in turn, this paid for a wall to enclose Monmouth against aggressors and vagrants. The charter details goods such as salt, beans, various cloths and woollens, honey, cider and copper, to name just a few. The charter was for five years and renewed in 1315 for another three years by King Edward II. The burgesses duly erected a town wall and gates, with today's Monnow Bridge and tower of Dixton gate being the only survivors.

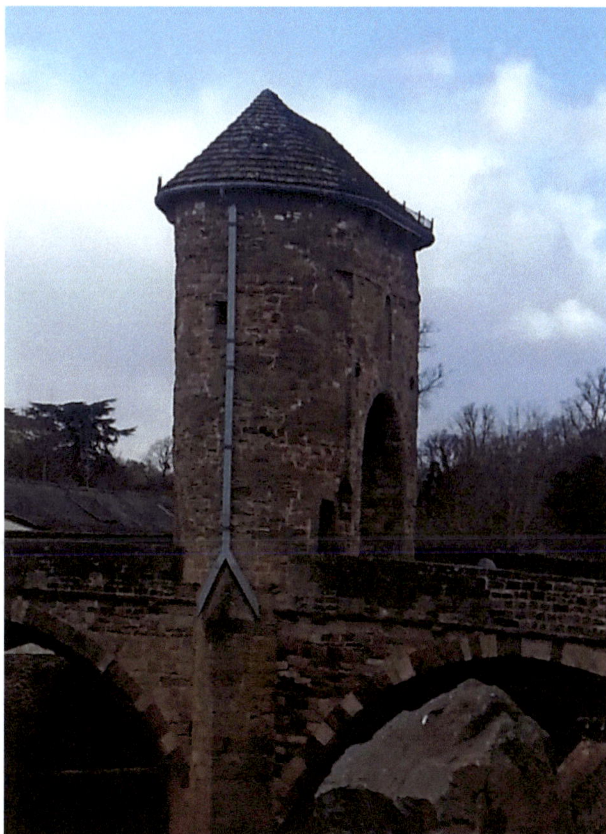

Monnow Bridge would have been made of wood originally. The stone one today dates from the late 1200s and the gatehouse to around 1300, although much rebuilding of the gatehouse has occurred over the years to become what we can see today.

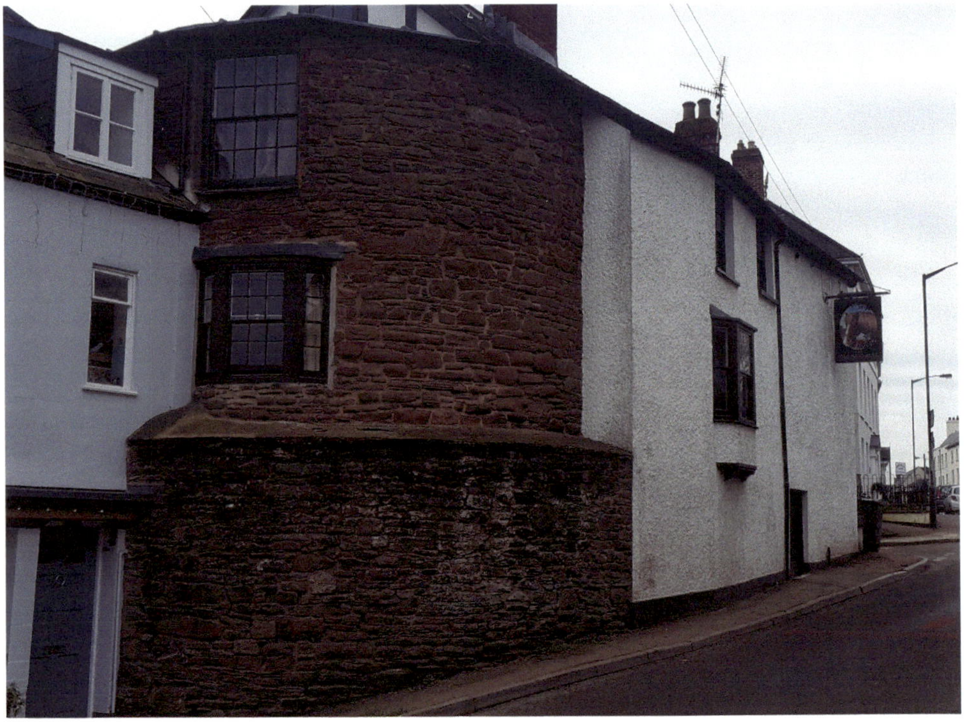

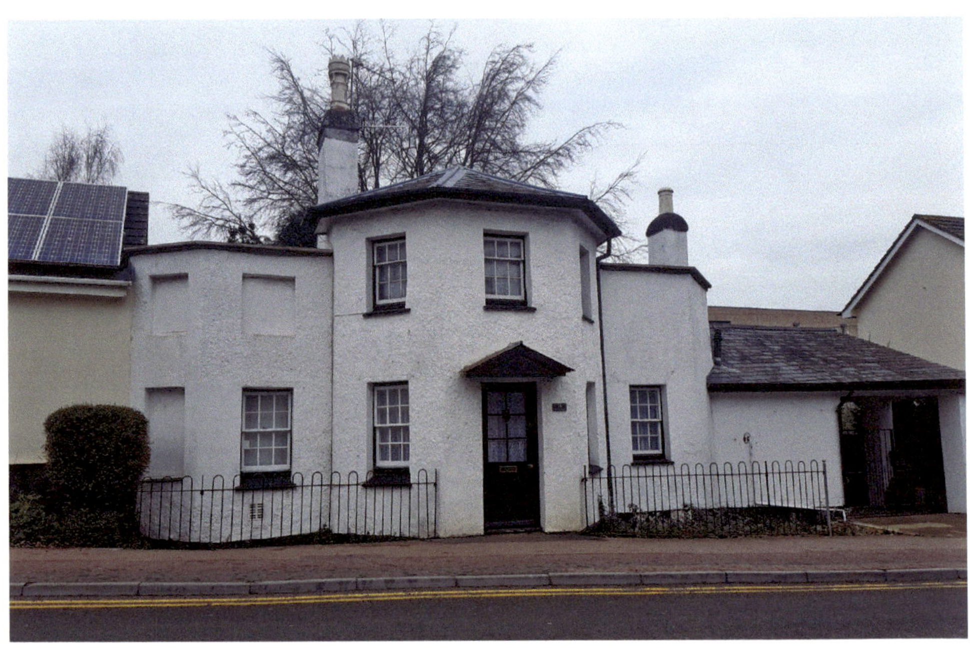

Above and Below: Top of Old Dixton Road, the tower remains of the medieval Dixton Gate, adjoining the Nags Head pub. This was also the area of the Roman road associated with Monmouth as mentioned in a previous chapter and heading from Caerleon to Hereford. Below is the Grade II listed Toll House when Old Dixton Road was the main turnpike road, opposite the Dixton Gate remains and dating from the early nineteenth century.

South Wales had much trade with Gloucester in medieval times. In 1378, Gloucester complained about their traders being unfairly distained when travelling into South Wales (this meant trader's goods were seized for money owed). However, the River Severn crossing at Gloucester into Wales was seen as Gloucester's major asset as by 1505 its trading with Wales was seen as one of its most stable economic elements.

We saw the importance of the River Wye as a trade and communication highway earlier. Boatbuilding along Monmouth Quay produced smaller 'trows', flat-bottomed boats that could be dragged up the muddy banks with masts that could be lowered so the trow could sail under the bridges. These boats carried stone and bark, which was the most important export in the mid-1800s, albeit seasonal. The bark was also the source of tannin for treating leather. In 1950, the Bristol Record Society published the document Records of Bristol Ships 1800–1838 (Vessels over 150 tons). It noted how, secondary to the large shipbuilding industry at Bristol, large ships were being built at Chepstow and further up the Wye. The *Monmouth*, a snow rig built in Monmouth, weighed 211 tonnes and nearly 89 feet in length. In his book *Monmouth: the Making of a County Town,* Kissack notes the short-lived industry of large shipbuilding in Monmouth due to the capsizing of the *Monmouth* as it was launched opposite the mouth of the River Monnow. However, the Records of Bristol Ships show how the *Monmouth* was lost at sea off Cuba in 1852. They do mention, however, a brig that was launched in Monmouth but lurched and several people were thrown overboard resulting in two boys drowning. Whatever happened, it signalled the end of larger shipbuilding in Monmouth.

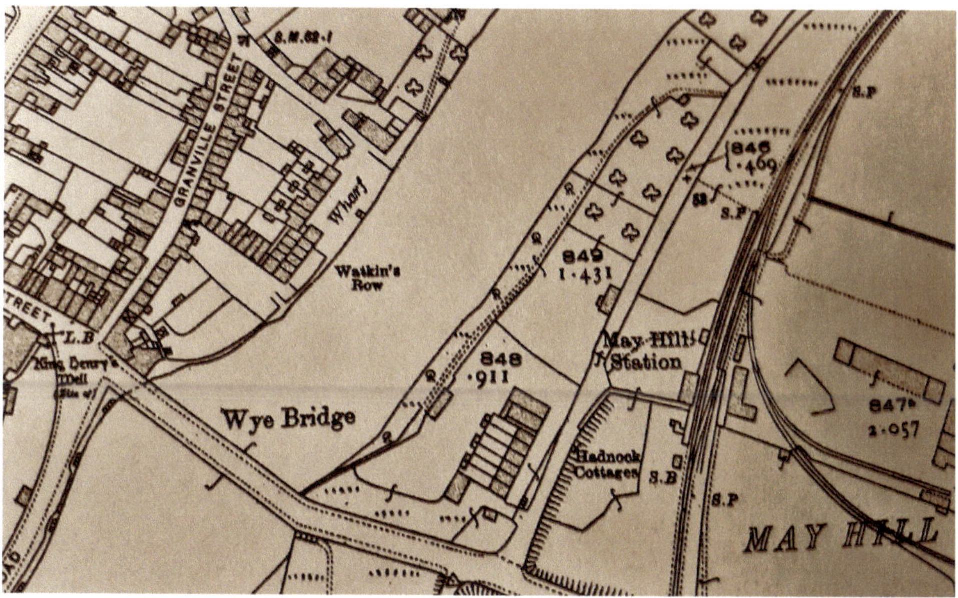

The wharf on the 1918 OS map. The port and associated warehouses and wharves were destroyed to make way for the new A40 relief road we see today.

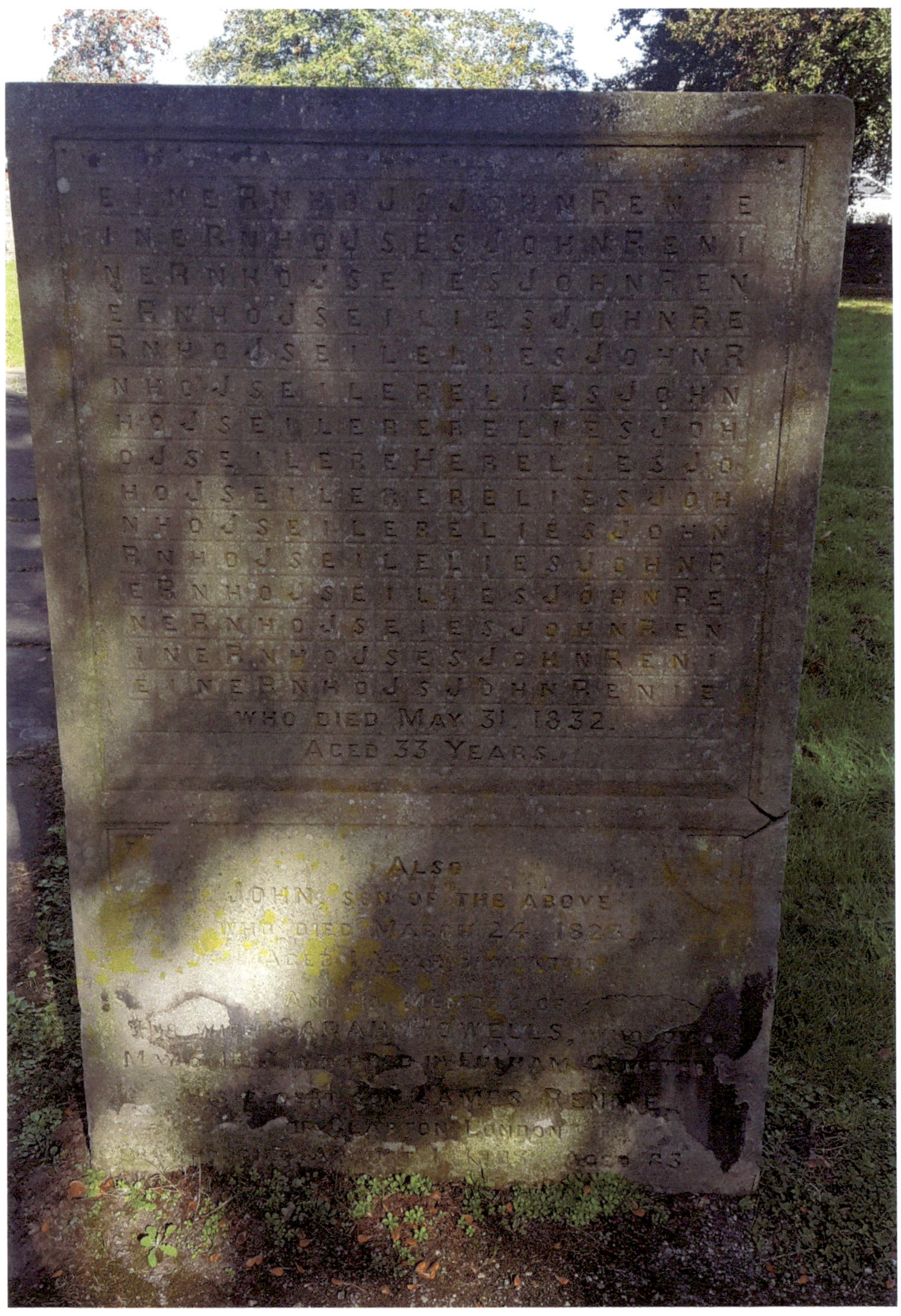

This Grade II listed memorial stone in St Mary's Graveyard is that of John Renie, a house painter who died in 1832 aged just thirty-three years old. He had carved this before his death, a 285-letter puzzle that reads 'Here lies John Renie' in every direction, thought to confuse the devil and thus have a safe passage to heaven.

The Monmouth Cap

Despite various sources quoting Overmonnow being known as Cappers Town, there is no mention of this in contemporary records. Although Monmouth Caps were not worn at Agincourt, the roll of names fighting under the Duke of Gloucester at Agincourt in 1415 included a Thomas Capper, a name prominent in Monmouth over the next 200 years or so. The cap itself was a cottage industry, and in 1523 Kissack notes the leasing of a house in Monnow Street by a Mr Thomas Capper, although the Monmouth Cap isn't mentioned until 1548 due to court records and disputes. One of these disputes was about a broken agreement on the teaching of knitting hats, which is allegedly one of the earliest mentions of knitting and may explain why the Monmouth Cap came to be revered as it was knitted, not made of leather or cloth. By design, it was a snug fit and was popular with the navy. In 1595/6, Exchequer Accounts for the last voyage of Francis Drake to the West Indies showed:

Monmouth Caps 16 doz at 26/a doz and 20 doz at 20/- a doz amount to £40.16.0
   At that time, Monmouth Caps therefore cost more than a pair of shoes, a shirt or linen breeches but less that worsted or wool stockings. Monmouth Museum, which displays the only known sixteenth century original cap to survive.

The manufacture of these woollen caps was moved to Bewdley in Worcestershire as the Black Death hit Monmouth, decimating the population, as was happening all over in Western Europe. Although there seems to be little documented about the plague in Wales, John Davies in his *History of Wales* notes that Wales had an approximate population of 300,000 in 1300; by 1400, it barely had 200,000. The plague probably hit Wales on two fronts: from the ports at Bristol and Gloucester as well as north-west via Shropshire when it hit Abergavenny. Monmouth's decimation is recorded on the ceramic memorial by Monnow Bridge.

DID YOU KNOW?
In 1394, a wealthy draper from Gloucester by the name of Richard Barret was attacked on the road through Monmouth to Usk.

Monmouth was originally in part of the ancient area called Archenfield (*Erging* in Welsh but there are various spellings), which stretched from Monmouth to Hereford and is now the area we know as southern Herefordshire. Within this area, the monks at Leominster grazed their sheep on fields of rye and the wool became known as being of exceptional quality – Ryeland sheep. Apparently, Elizabeth I was given a gift of Lemster stockings and approved the quality so much, she insisted on having Ryeland wool thereafter. Monmouth's position on an arterial river and trading with the large port of Bristol, coupled with access to high-quality wool, it can be of no surprise that

The ceramic table highlighting Monmouth's history.

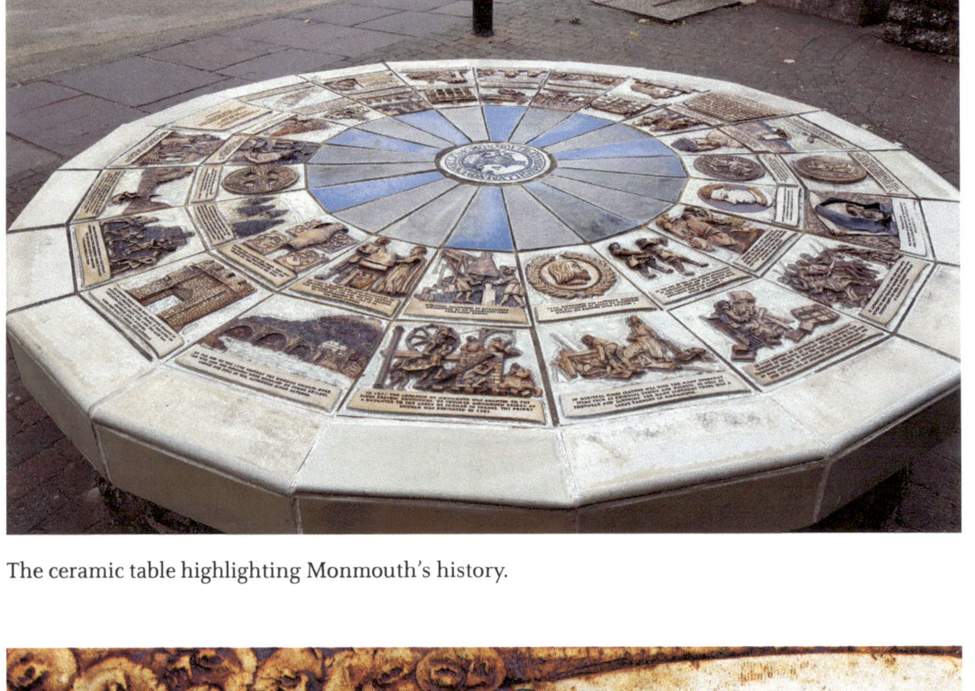

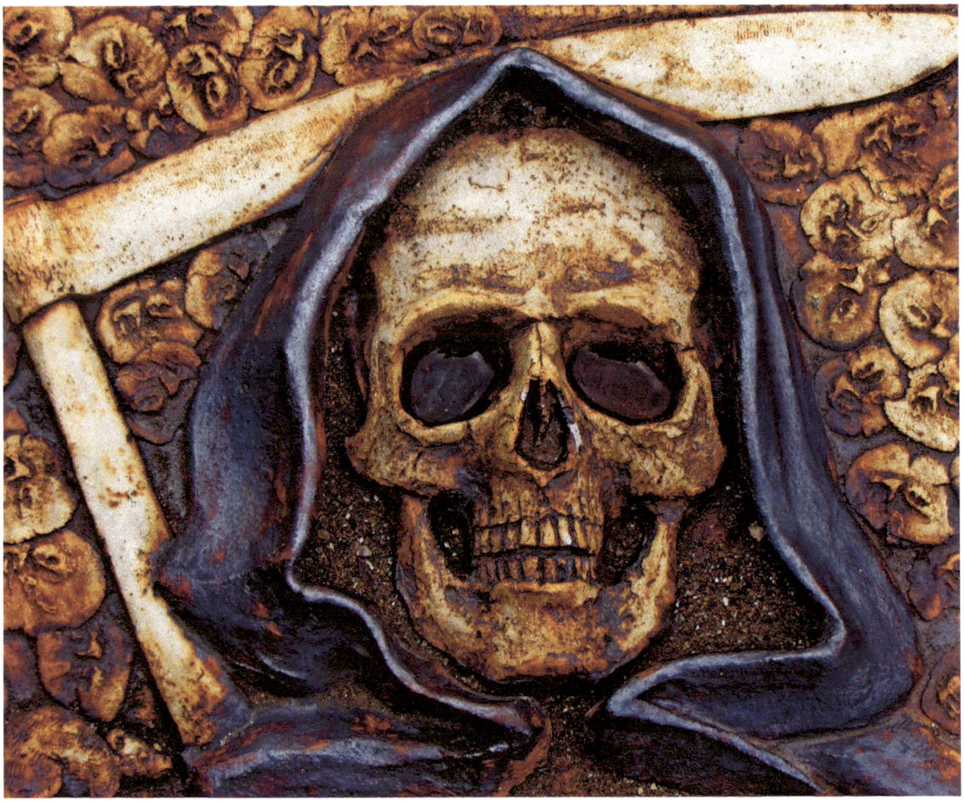

A close-up of the tile representing Monmouth being decimated by the plague in 1349 and 1369. (Image courtesy of Leo Reynolds under Creative Commons 2.0)

a high-quality knitted cap, possibly using Ryeland wool among others, came from Monmouth and spread throughout the world.

Textile manufacturing and trading, along with groceries, was common in Monmouth. In 1895, Kelly's Directory listed the following in Monnow Street alone:

Frederick Ackland, draper and milliner, 54 and 93 Monnow Street
Richard Adams, grocer, 92 Monnow Street
Mrs Amelia Dew, milliner and dressmaker, 90 Monnow Street
Thomas Howse, clothier and outfitter, 35 Monnow Street
James Rudge Barrel, grocer, 34 Monnow Street
Alfred Basham, grocer, 55 Monnow Street
Charles Farror, corn and flour dealer, 16 Monnow Street

Kelly's Directory goes onto list the successful market that had been in existence since the Middle Ages, a cattle market (where the car park and toilets at the bottom of Monnow Street are now) that opened in 1876, nail-making (hence the road called Nailers Lane), a tannery and charcoal forges in Monmouth, also mentioned by William Coxe in his writings *An Historical Tour in Monmouthshire* in 1801 as being owned by the Messrs Harford, Partridge & Co. There was also a wool fair held on the second Monday in February, in May, Whitsun Tuesday, and second Monday in September and November.

DID YOU KNOW?
A son of Tintern, Colonel Lewis Morris fought for Oliver Cromwell and was allegedly second in command during the Parliamentary attack on Chepstow Castle. At the Restoration of Charles II, he left for his family estates in Barbados and then to America to care for his nephew after the death of his brother Richard. The colonel bought great tracts of land in the area that became Monmouth County, including iron and corn mills. He named his holdings Tintern Manor after his family lands in Wales that hand been confiscated by Charles II. The area is today known as Tinton Falls. His nephew grew up to be Governor of New Jersey and Morristown was named after him.

DID YOU KNOW?
Abbey Forge at Tintern was the first place that brass was made in Britain and the first to make wire on an industrial scale. The first transatlantic cable was made in Tintern.

Monmouth's prosperity – and lack of – has undulated over the years. Today, one can see the fine houses. It had its trades, agriculture and markets but all suffered over the years due to working conditions, fluctuating trade and so on. Daniel Defoe, the author of *Robinson Crusoe*, is also known as the father of modern journalism. His three-volume travel book, *Tour Through the Whole Island of Great Britain*, was written between 1724 and 1727 and was regarded as innovative as Defoe actually visited the places he wrote about. Part of this travel writing involved Monmouth in 1726, with Defoe finding it rather 'decayed':

From hence we came at about 8 miles more into Monmouthshire, and to the town of Monmouth. It is an old town situate at the conflux of the Wye and of Munnow, whence the town has its name; it stands in the angle where the rivers joyn, and has a bridge over each river, and a third over the River Trothy, which comes in just below the other.

This town shews by its reverend face, that it is a place of great antiquity, and by the remains of walls, lines, curtains, and bastions, that it has been very strong, and by its situation that it may be made so again: This place is made famous, by being the native place of one of our most antient historians Jeoffry of Monmouth. At present 'tis rather a decay'd than a flourishing town, yet, it drives a considerable trade with the city of Bristol, by the navigation of the Wye.

This river having as I said, just received two large streams, the Mynevly or Munno, and the Trother, is grown a very noble river, and with a deep chanel, and a full current hurries away towards the sea, carrying also vessels of a considerable burthen hereabouts.

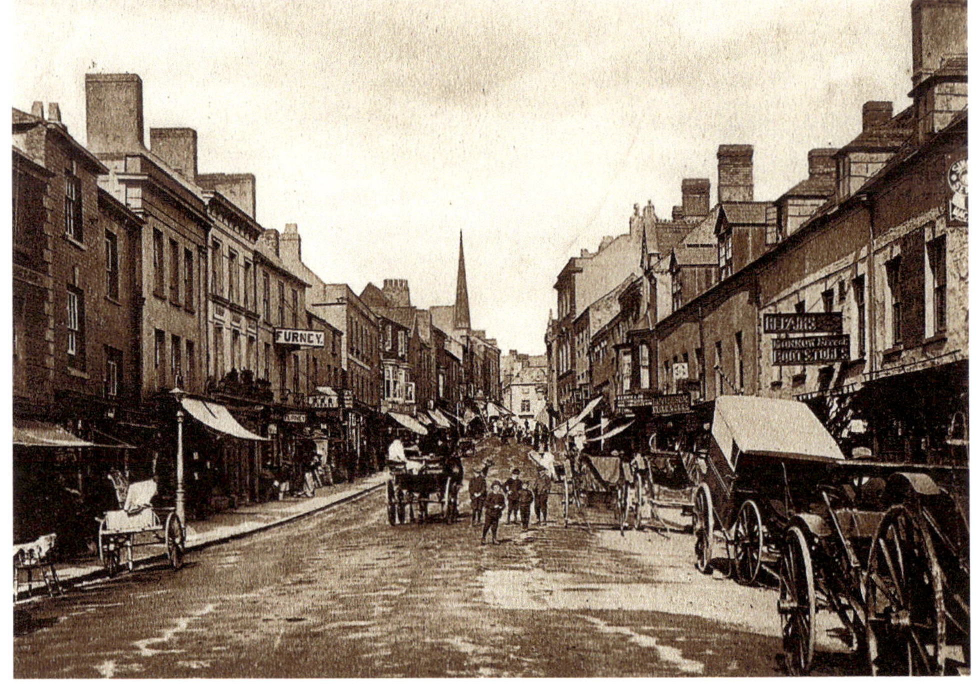

Monnow Street, 1918.

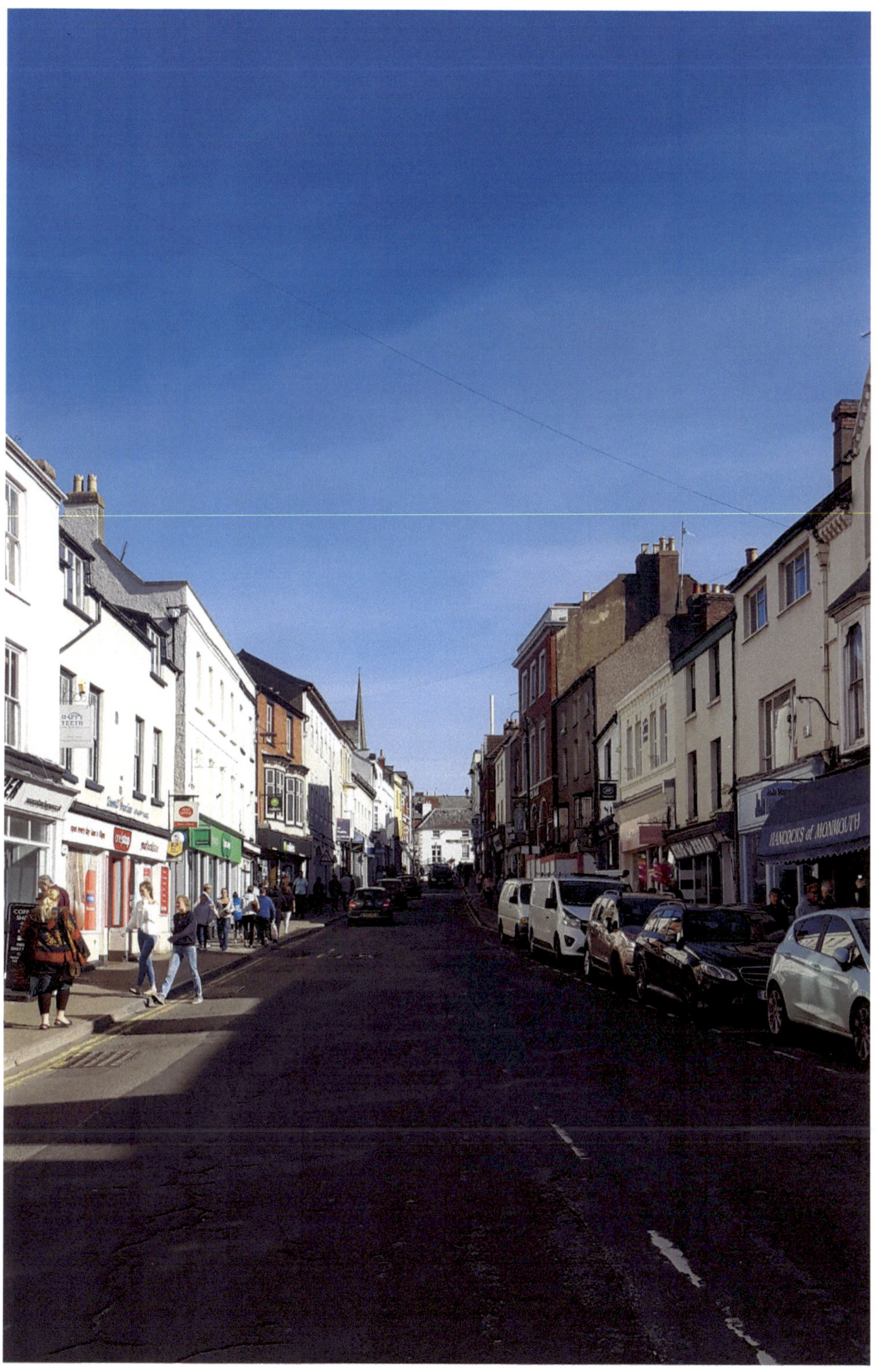

Monnow Street, 2018.

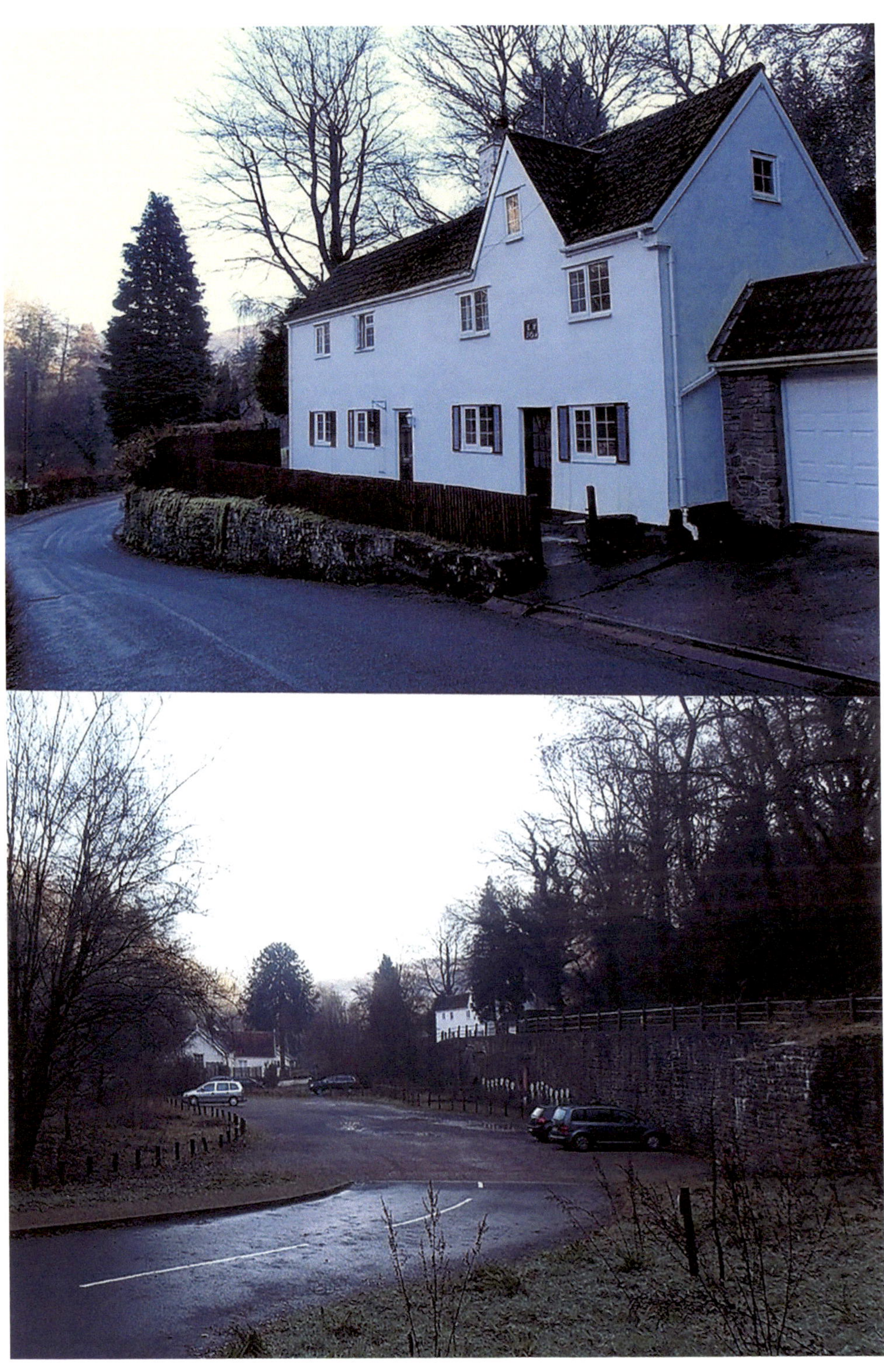

Lower Wireworks House, now residential and dating from the late seventeenth century, and Lower Wireworks car park. (Images courtesy of Jaggery under Creative Commons 2.0)

4. The Lordship of Monmouth

One of the very few people that can be proven to have fought in the Battle of Hastings in October 1066 was William FitzOsbern. Childhood friend and distant kin of the Conqueror, FitzOsbern was the Conqueror's right-hand man during the aftermath of the Norman invasion. This included the building of many castles, especially within Wales, to protect routes, land, borders and as a sign of their power and influence.

FitzOsbern is probably remembered best for his magnificent Chepstow Castle. However, he also built Monmouth and it is believed, but not proven, he also built the nearby Three Castles – Skenfrith, White Castle and Grosmont. These were all originally in the wooden format of motte and bailey castles and the last three guarded the route of Wales to Hereford at the time. White Castle is the better preserved of the three and was originally called Llantilio Castle due to the nearby village it looked over.

DID YOU KNOW?
Bretons were people from Brittany, France, who were descended from the settlers who migrated in waves from south-west England (mainly Devon and Cornwall) during the Anglo-Saxon invasion of England, namely between the third and ninth centuries. The area they settled in, Brittany, was named after them.

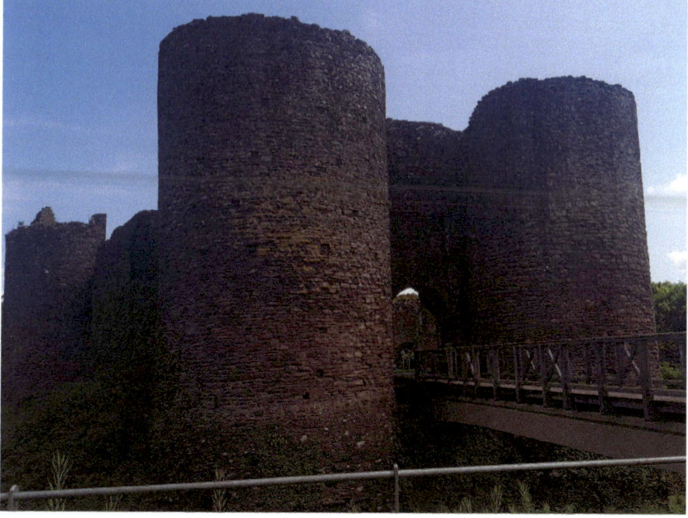

Approach to White Castle from the outer bailey. The earliest remains are the twelfth-century curtain walls. The castle was fortified in the thirteenth century.

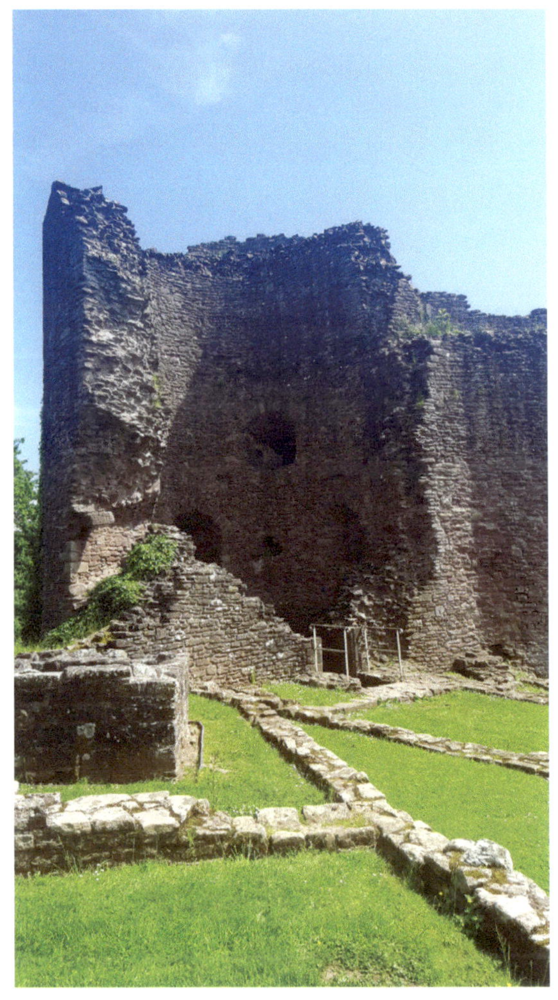

Inner bailey of White Castle with
remains of the well, kitchen and chapel.

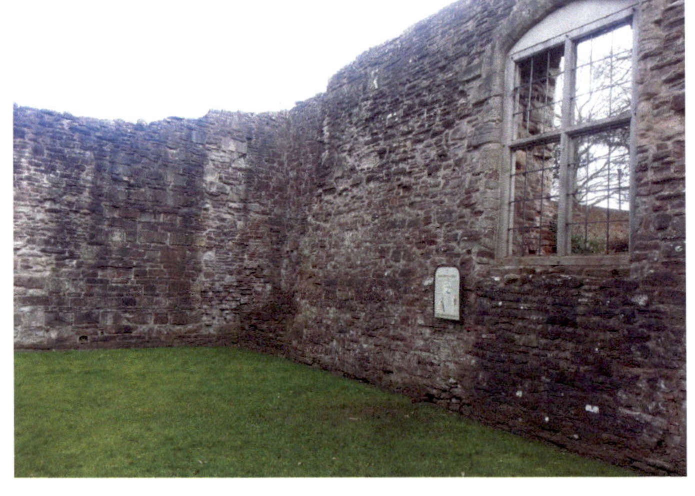

Remains of the Great Hall,
Monmouth Castle.

Monmouth was built at the confluence of the rivers Wye and Monnow and Chepstow stood guard over the Wye and Severn, all extremely valuable river trade routes, allowing access to the Forest of Dean and the thriving Anglo-Saxon cities of Gloucester and Hereford, not to mention accessibility to Bristol and the River Severn and beyond. According to David Sivier in his book *Anglo-Saxon and Norman Bristol*, twenty-four of the new towns built by the Normans were on the coast/rivers for ease of supplies from England. FitzOsbern used Bristol to supply Chepstow, his base for driving his power through South East Wales, decimating Gwent. He also built wooden structures at Wigmore, Clifford and Ewyas Harold and all of these castles were later rebuilt in stone.

The Norman Marcher lords, and notably FitzOsbern, were right to be on guard. Although the Welsh knew their territory and fought passionately, they were no match for the organised Norman warrior. The Anglo-Saxon Chronicle tells us how the river, while good for trade, was also a way in for those not prepared to be under Norman rule:

Amidst this came one of Harold's sons from Ireland with a naval force into the mouth of the Avon unawares, and plundered soon over all that quarter; whence they went to Bristol, and would have stormed the town; but the people bravely withstood them. (Anglo-Saxon Chronicle, 1067–69)

All that we see today of Monmouth Castle are the remains of two interlocking rooms, the Great Tower and Great Hall. It has been an assize court, the town gaol, a girls' school and is the home of the longest-serving militia, which is discussed – along with later history of the castle – in the chapter Crime and Punishment. Today's Agincourt Square was the market place that grew from the original bailey of Monmouth Castle and was originally much bigger. The lordship of Monmouth passed to the younger John of Monmouth in 1248, who only held the title and the castle until 1256 where he passed his lands and properties to Prince Edward, son of Henry III. Kissack, in his *Medieval Monmouth,* states it is not known whether the younger John of Monmouth passed his lordship and all that entails due to illness as he died the following year, or debt. The latter is the most likely reason.

The castle later passed to Edward's younger brother, Prince Edmund (also known as Crouchback, not for physical reasons but allegedly meaning 'cross-back', the cross stitched into his cloak referring to his participation in the Ninth Crusade), 1st Earl of Lancaster, and so begun the Lancastrian lordship of Monmouth. Edmund's great-great-great-grandson would be Henry V, who was born in Monmouth Castle in 1386.

FitzOsbern, according to *The History of Monmouthshire Vol 4, Part 1* by Sir Joseph Bradney (himself a High Sheriff of Monmouthshire in 1899), went on the offensive in southern Gwent and the Forest of Dean but no recorded tales of battle exist. This would lend to the idea that hardly any opposition reared up to the encroaching Normans and FitzOsbern went on to build Monmouth Castle, Hereford, Ewyas Harold, Clifford and Wigmore. The Conqueror did not encourage his men to raid further into Wales but neither did he stop them; Davies notes in his *History of Wales* that by 1081 however, William had no intention of annexing Wales and it appeared none of the kingdoms of Wales had much future. By 1086, the superiority of the Norman invaders of south-east Wales was

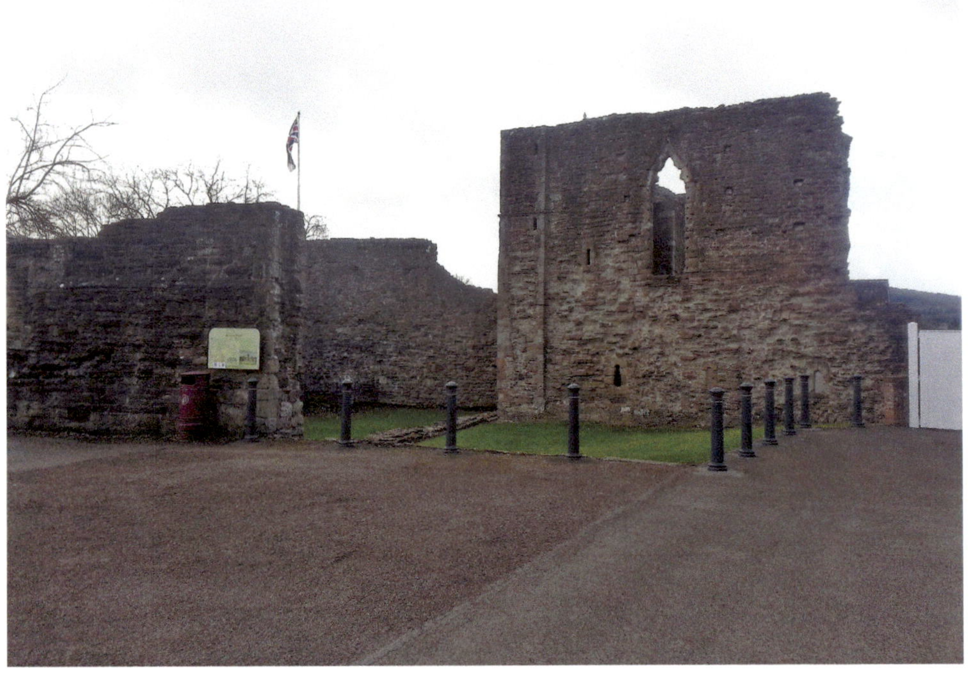

Above: The approach to the remains of
Monmouth Castle.

Right: Gatehouse remains of the castle
where Henry V was born.

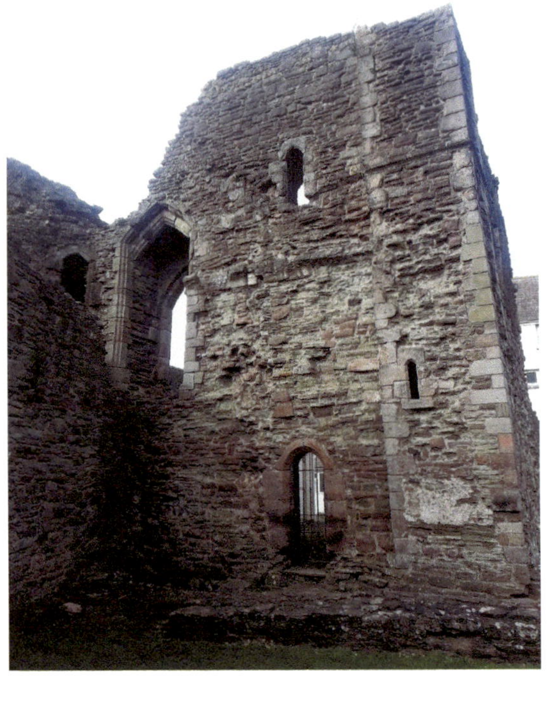

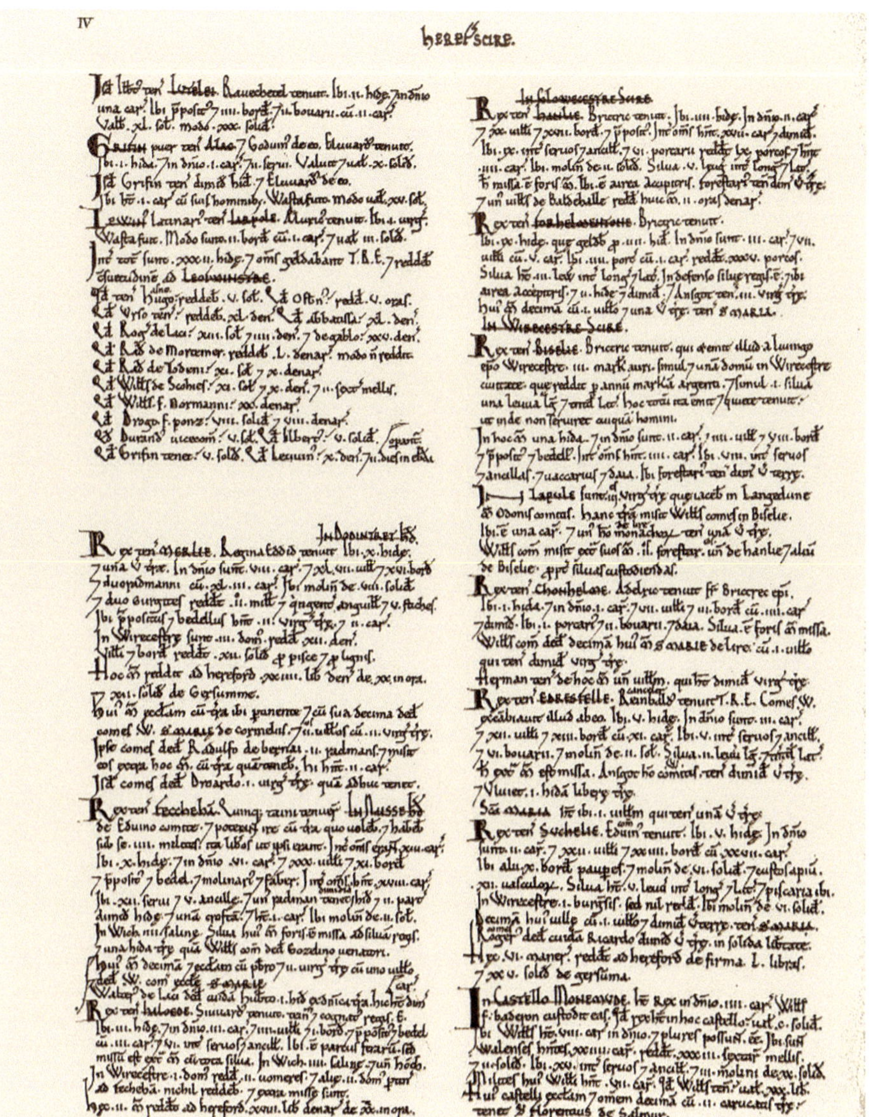

Domesday Book, 1086. Note how Monmouth (last paragraph in right-hand column) is under Herefordshire; it lists the following information:

'Total population: 15 households (medium). Only the head of the family was counted so the real figure is probably much higher.

Taxable units: Taxable value 2 carucates units. Taxed on 2.0. Payments of 0.1 customary.

Value: Value to lord in 1086 £35.

Households: 8 slaves. 7 female slaves.

Ploughland: 12 lord's plough teams. 31 men's plough teams.

Other resources: 3 mills, value 1.0. 1 church. 2.0 church lands.

Lord in 1066: King Edward

Lords in 1086: King William; William son of Baderon

Tenant-in-chief in 1086: King William.'

(Image courtesy of Professor John Palmer, George Slater at opendomesday.org)

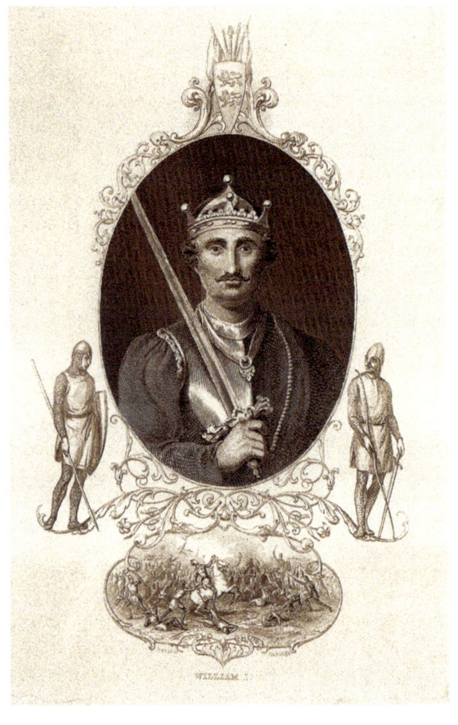

No picture appears to exist of William FitzOsbern, but maybe one of the figures above next to William the Conqueror is based on him. (Image courtesy of the Wellcome Collection)

showing – they had established castles at Chepstow, Monmouth and Caerleon, as shown in the Domesday Book; William FitzOsbern had also managed to crush the kingdom of Gwent. Davies notes that although the Welsh knew their land inside out and had had mounted warriors for generations, not only did the Normans have superior armour, horses and arms, they were 'colonists of genius'. *Secret Chepstow* (Wyatt, 2018)

Late 1070/early 1071, FitzOsbern, as one of William the Conqueror's most trusted men, was sent by the Conqueror on an errand to help the Conqueror's wife, Matilda, govern Normandy and assist a neighbouring nobleman in a territorial war. In February 1071, FitzOsbern and his party of ten knights were ambushed and he was killed, his body being carried to the abbey in Cormeilles, Normandy, that he founded in 1060, where he was buried. One of his sons, Roger de Breutil, became 2nd Earl of Hereford but inherited much reduced land, property and estates than his father had enjoyed. He became known as one of the earls in the Revolt of the Earls in 1075, along with his brother-in-law Ralph de Gael, Earl of East Anglia, and Earl Walthof, Earl of Northumberland. According to the sources, William the Conqueror refused permission for Ralph de Gael to marry Emma, daughter of FitzOsbern and sister to Roger. As he was away in Normandy, William refused to sanction the marriage but Roger gave permission and they went ahead with the marriage anyway. It was at the wedding celebrations that all three earls decided to revolt. It seems the fact that all three had inherited much less than what had been their fathers led to the rebellion. However, it wasn't well supported and Earl Waltheof had a change of heart and confessed to the plan. Roger was apprehended by a fyrd (a militia force of freemen of that county) before he could even cross the River Severn and was sentenced to life imprisonment; Ralph escaped by ship to Breton and was later joined by his wife Emma; and Waltheof was beheaded in 1076. All three were disinherited of their lands and possessions and any custodians of Monmouth Castle who were involved in the revolt were removed, with temporary custodianship given to Ranulf de Colville. It was the last known uprising against the Conqueror.

DID YOU KNOW?
William de Braose lured Welsh princes and leaders to Abergavenny Castle in 1175 on the pretence of making peace. He had them all killed and in retaliation, a Welsh lord of Caerleon destroyed Dingestow Castle (approximately 4 miles south-west of Monmouth) and burnt Abergavenny Castle.

In 1075, the next 200 years of Breton lordship arrived with Gwethenoc (sometimes spelt Withenoc), a nobleman and monk. King William rewarded Bretons who had supported his invasion of England and his advancement to add Wales to his conquered lands, settling many of them on the land. Monmouth was one such estate. It is supposed that the famous writer of this era, Geoffrey of Monmouth, could have been part of this Breton entourage or had familial links with Gwethenoc but he will be discussed in a later chapter.

In 1080, Gwethenoc founded Monmouth Priory but gave up his secular life in 1082 and retired as a monk to the abbey in Samur, France. There have been archaeological remains found on the site, especially *tesserae*, which would have formed a mosaic in a high-status Roman building. Sources say that St Mary's Church, next to the priory, is built on the site of an eight-century church dedicated to St Cadoc, which is also suggested in the Liber Llandavensis (better known as the Book of Llandaff, a twelfth-century chartulary/register of the cathedral church Llandaff). Therefore, there has probably been worship on the site for time immemorial.

Gwethenoc returned to Monmouth in 1101 to see the priory consecrated. At this point in time, the priory would have had access to the river down the bank and overlooked the flood plains.

As Gwethenoc's son and brother were also monks, Monmouth Castle passed to his brother's son, William FitzBaderon, the new lord of Monmouth as well as at least ten other manors surrounding Monmouth. It is FitzBaderon we see as lord of the manor in the Domesday Book of 1086, which also shows Monmouth and its environs as being a flourishing agricultural community and it is thought it was FitzBaderon who completed the stone building of the castle.

In 1125, his son, Baderon FitzWilliam (1100–76) became lord of Monmouth around 1125 and sometime after 1130 married the daughter of the rival family at Chepstow, Rohesia de Clare, and this union helped alleviate anxieties around Monmouth due to the power of the de Clare family. Rohesia became known for her generosity to Monmouth Priory, bestowing much financial assistance; Baderon's sister, Margaret, also donated generously to Monmouth. It was through marriage that Rohesia of Monmouth would become the great-great-aunt of Richard Marshal, Earl of Pembroke and lord of Chepstow, who in turn would be the instigator of the Battle of Monmouth in 1233.

DID YOU KNOW?
Edward II stayed over at Monmouth Castle as a prisoner on his doomed journey to Berkeley Castle.

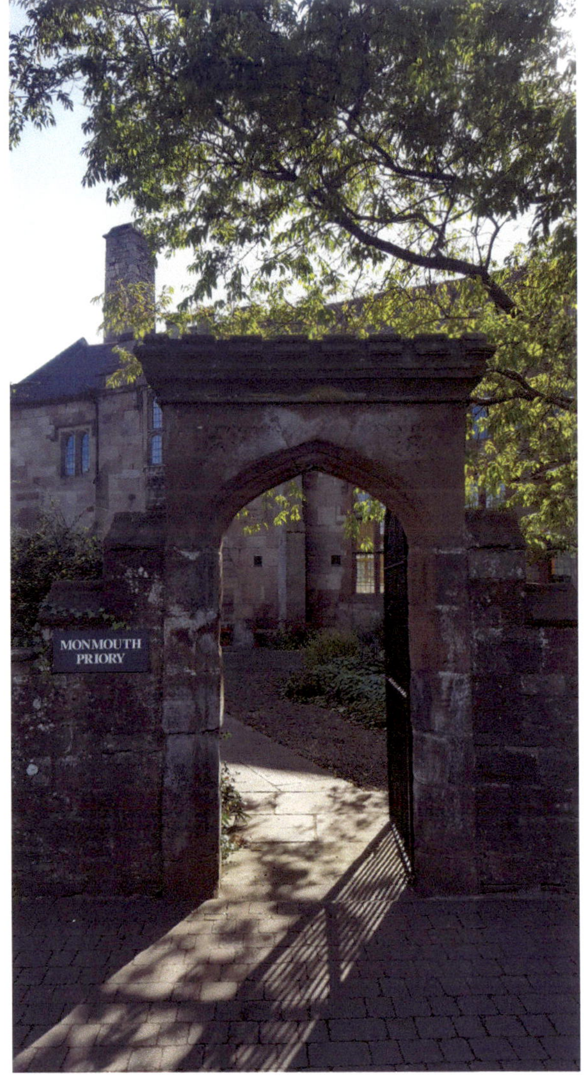

Entrance on Priory Street.

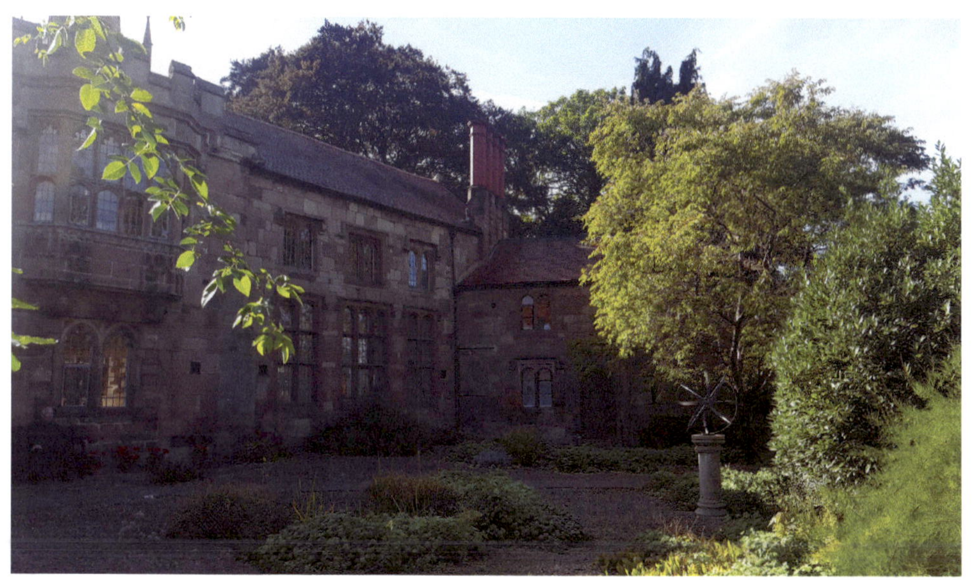

View to Priory Street entrance with Castle Field (Vauxhall Fields) beyond the car park.

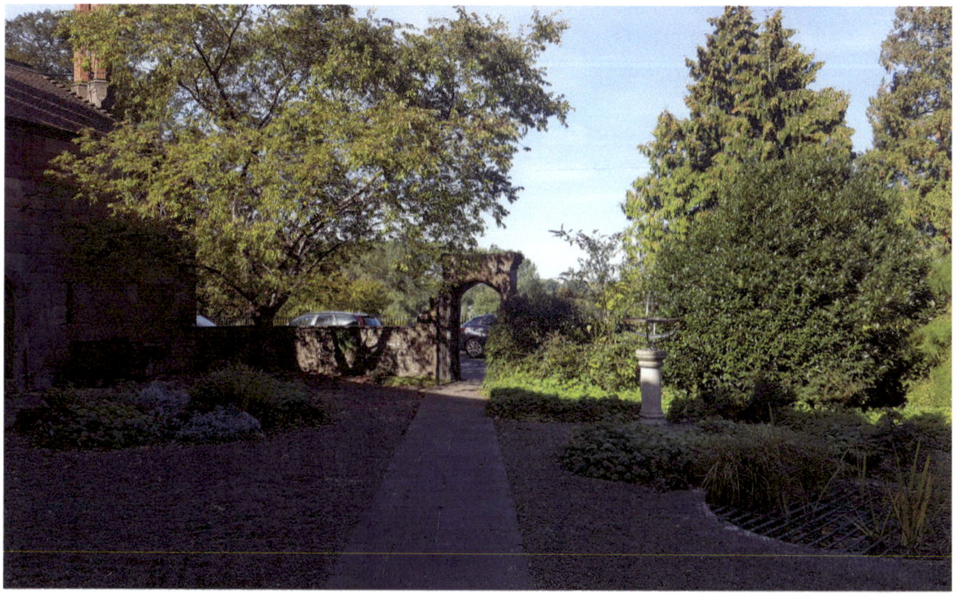

Monmouth Priory courtyard, founded by Gwethenoc in 1080. Top left of the photograph is the bay window known as Geoffrey's Window, named after Geoffrey of Monmouth, who is discussed in a later chapter.

Baderon and Rohesia's son, Gilbert, became lord of Monmouth in 1172 and was married to Bertha. It was their son, John of Monmouth, who would become a favourite of King John and Henry III while holding the Monmouth title for nearly fifty years.

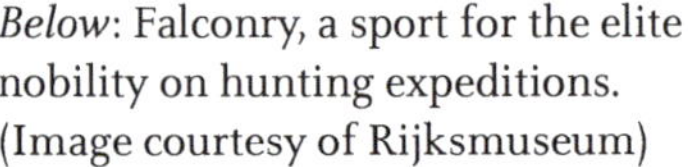

Right: Icelandic Gyrfalcon from a 1759 painting.

Below: Falconry, a sport for the elite nobility on hunting expeditions. (Image courtesy of Rijksmuseum)

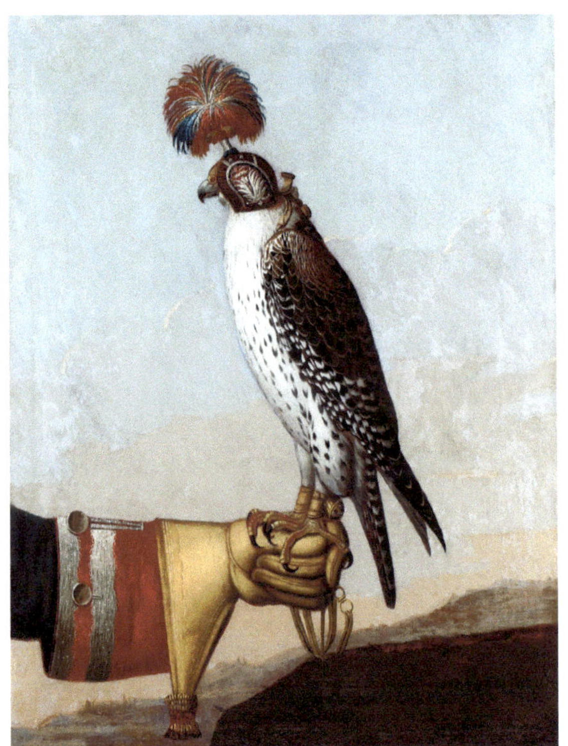

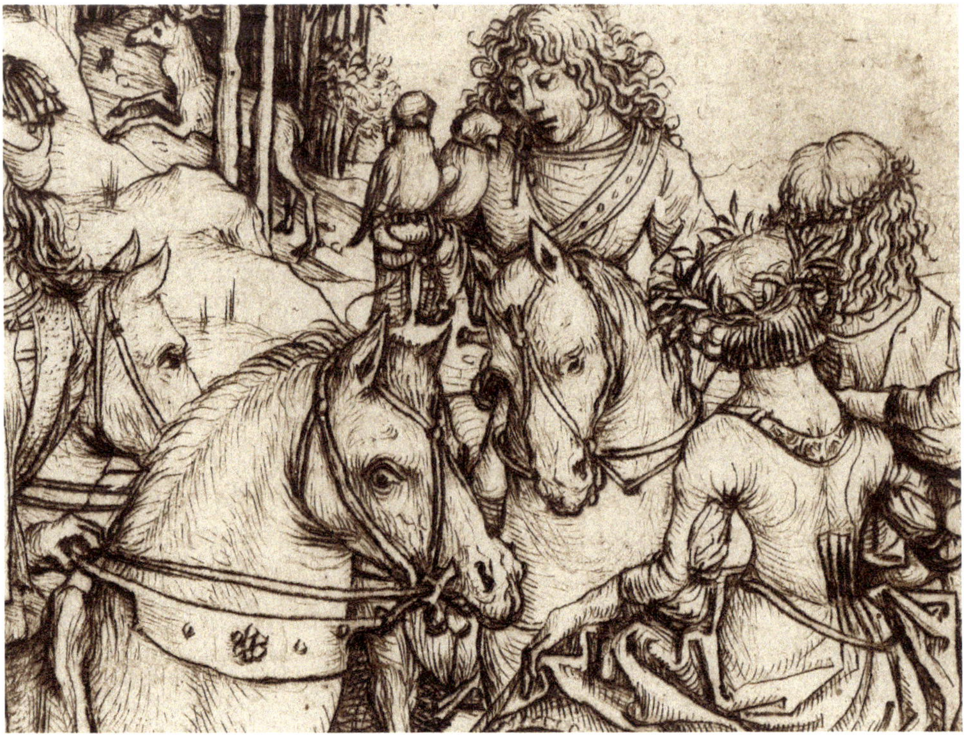

John of Monmouth

John (*c.* 1182–1248) was too young to take up the lordship of Monmouth when his father died around 1189/90 so was made a ward of his uncle, William de Braose, a powerful Marcher lord of Abergavenny, Brecknock, Builith and Limerick, to name just a few.

By 1205 he had come of age and had married Cecily, the daughter of Walter de Waleran, by 1201, for whom he had partly paid with two gyrfalcons to King John for her share of her fathers' lands. Falconry had been extremely popular for hunting in England since the Saxon king of Kent, Ethelbert II, and had risen to be a status symbol. Gyrfalcons were introduced by the Normans after 1066 and were extremely valuable, as they are today.

Cecily died in 1222 and he then married Agnes, daughter of Walter de Musgros. There seems to be some confusion with some sources regarding John of Monmouth's heir, also called John; some say he was the son of Cecily, some say Agnes, but whoever it was, the younger John of Monmouth would be Monmouth's surviving heir and would be the last Breton lord.

John of Monmouth became a favourite and loyal servant to King John and, in turn, his heir Henry III. King John had visited Monmouth briefly in 1213 on a hunting expedition and a mere three years later, Monmouth was at King John's bedside as he died and was one of the executors of his will. Monmouth received further promotion when Henry III then took the throne.

In 1229, John granted a hermitage (a small and isolated dwelling for a hermit) called The Garth to a hospital he had founded. Gwent and Glamorgan Archaeological Trust (GGAT) state not only it is unclear to what hospital the grant refers to but John of Monmouth founded a later hospital in 1240 to St John, which was given to Monmouth Priory by his son. Stephen Clarke, in his book *Down the Dig*, also notes Chapel Farm, which was on the site of a medieval hospital named St Michael, was possibly founded by John of Monmouth and slightly upstream on an ancient crossing of the river from the Forest of Dean. The site is now under the bypass.

DID YOU KNOW?
Erging (and Gwent) are the areas where the ancient Llandaff diocese was allegedly initiated by Dubricus, an evangelist. Criticism of these claims of early foundations of Llandaff include the irregular and questionable copying in the twelfth century of the original sixth-century texts.

John of Monmouth also found a Cistercian abbey called Grace Dieu in Monmouth on what was probably the west bank of the River Trothy, approximately 2 miles north of Dingestow. It was relocated after being destroyed in 1233, possibly on the east side of the River Trothy. There is a farm called Parc-Grace Dieu near the area where the abbey is thought to have been and although no remains survive at least above ground, there are some linear features in Abbey Meadow that could be related, but to date it is inconclusive.

Grace Dieu had the sad reputation of being one of the poorest and smallest abbeys in Britain with a rather tragic history, probably due to its tenuous geographical position in the border lands of Wales and England coupled with bad management. Below is a short timeline of Grace Dieu adapted from Monastic Wales (http://www.monasticwales.org).

Date	History Timeline of Grace Dieu Abbey, Monmouth
1217	John of Monmouth requests permission to found a Cistercian abbey
24 April 1226	Grace Dieu Abbey founded by a community sent from Dore Abbey in Herefordshire
1232	The abbot and a monk kidnapped by Welshmen, claiming the abbey has been built on their land and John of Monmouth had no right
1233	The abbey is destroyed by fighting forces in the Battle of Monmouth
1235	Henry III grants twenty trees from the Forest of Dean for the abbey to be rebuilt
1236	Possible relocation of abbey from the west bank of the River Trothy to the east
1240	Another grant of trees, this time oaks from Grosmont Forest, from Henry III to help with rebuilding
1253	Yet another grant of two oaks from Seinfremy/Seinfrenny Wood (unsure of this location)
1276	Possibility of another move due to local conflict
1291	The abbey had an estimated net income of £18 5s 8d (around £20,000 today), and approximately 729 ha of arable land, a mill that was rented out, twenty-two sheep and eight granges
1335	The abbot was excommunicated for non-payment
1351	Roger of Chepstow, abbot, resigned due to administration of the abbey and ongoing struggles with neighbours
1484	Another resignation from the abbot – John Mitulton – who, according to his contemporaries, was a 'good and honest man' but resigned due to persecution by his enemies
1536	Still having a low income much akin to previous amounts, the abbey fell victim to the Dissolution of the Monasteries and was dissolved on 3 September 1536

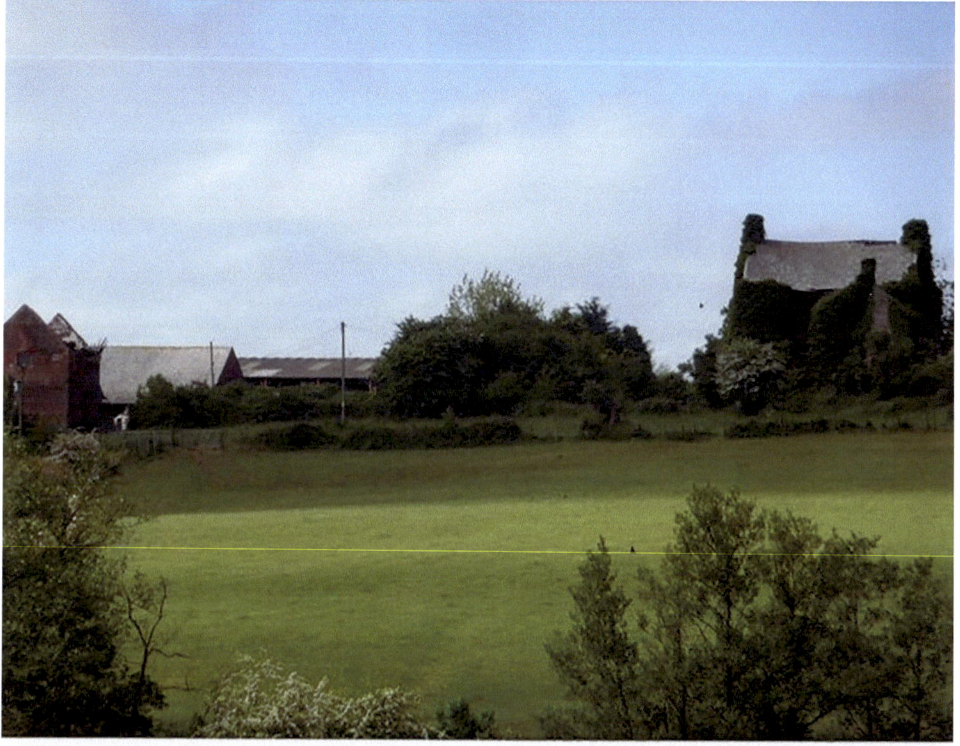

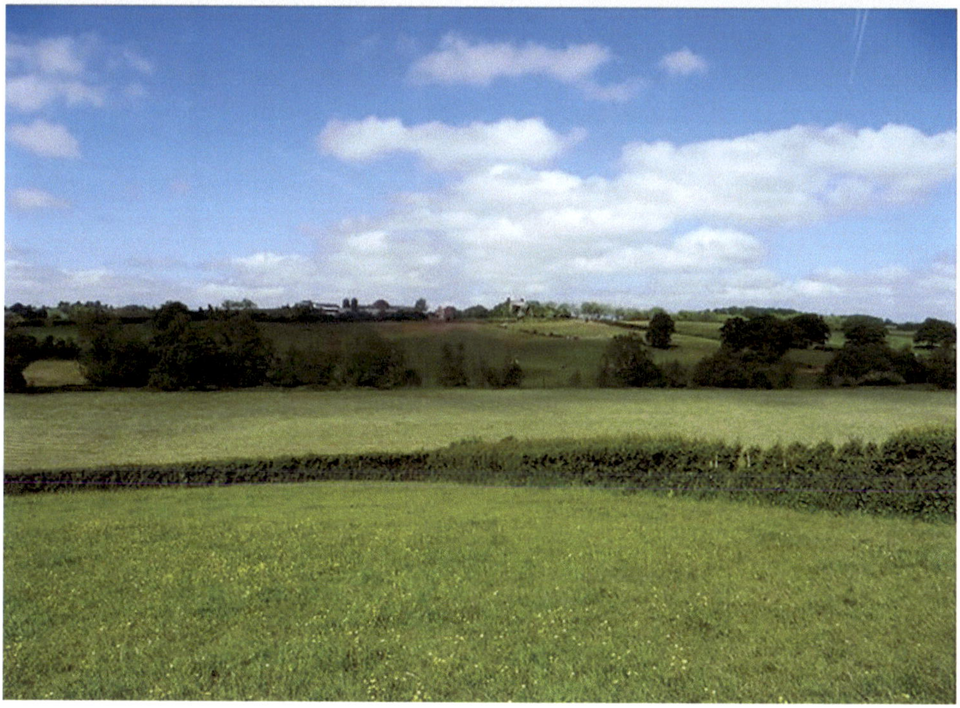

Parc Grace Dieu valley and farmhouse. (Images courtesy of Jeremy Bolwell under Creative Commons 2.0)

John of Monmouth, founder of possibly two hospitals (one mentioned by executor of Henry III's policies in South Wales), arbiter and advisor in Anglo-Welsh affairs, died in Monmouth in 1248 after nearly fifty years as the lord of Monmouth and was buried in St Mary's, Monmouth. Unfortunately, his tomb was destroyed during renovations in 1737.

Battle of Monmouth, 1233

Roger of Wendover (d. 1236) was a monk at St Albans Abbey, historian and prior of Belvoir, a Leicestershire cell of St Albans, and became one of the most notable English chroniclers of the thirteenth century. Wendover's writing has been criticised for inaccuracies and shallow writing but this could be due to the fact that comparisons to his successor as St Albans principal historian, the more famous Matthew Paris, is considered to have written a more interesting historiography. However, it is through his writings in *Flores Historiarum* (*Flowers of History*) that we know details of the Battle of Monmouth in November 1233, between Richard [the] Marshal, second son of the more famous William the Marshal, lord of Chepstow and Earl of Pembroke amongst many other titles, who was one of Britain's most famous and important historical characters.

Richard Marshal had a stormy relationship with Henry III, including refusing to pay a dower of his widowed sister-in-law who was also the king's sister, as well as rebelling against the influence of Poitevans in local government; a tangled web of politics, too complicated to include in this book, appears to have led to the Battle of Monmouth.

In November 1233, John of Monmouth was absent and the king had made Baldwin III, Count of Guines (now northern France), the castellan of Monmouth Castle. Baldwin was a mercenary Flemish nobleman but Richard Marshal also had mercenaries. The men that fought against Monmouth with him were the Marshal baronial leader Gilbert Bassett, who had married into the Marshal family, and Richard Siward, a thirteenth-century mercenary soldier who earned his knighthood by being a retainer of the Marshals. He married Gilbert's sister (or some sources say his cousin), Phillippa Bassett, the widowed Countess of Warwick, thus bringing Siward much land and wealth.

Both Siward and Gilbert had fallen into royal disfavour and sought shelter within the house of Richard Marshal. With all their grievances, all three finally rebelled. From Roger of Wendover's Flores Historiarum, we know that on the evening of 25 November 1233, Richard Marshal, who owned all the surrounding land and knew Monmouth was against him, was on a foraging expedition to check out the defences before planning to come back with a large force to besiege the castle. He was, however, spotted patrolling by Baldwin of Guines, who led a fighting force out into the fields. The brief but bloody encounter was described by Wendover as:

...and understanding that the marshal was there with only a few followers to examine the castle, he [Baldwin] sailed out with a thousand brave and well-equipped soldiers and pursued him at full speed, designing to make him and his followers prisoners and bring them into town. The earl Marshal's companions however, when they saw the impetuous advance of the enemy, advised him to consult their safety by flight, saying that it would be rash for such a few of them to engage with such a number of the enemy; to which the Marshal replied that he had never yet turned his back on his enemies in battle and declared that he would not do so now and exhorted them to defend themselves bravely and to not die unavenged. The troops from the castle then rushed fiercely on them and attacked them with their lances.

It was Richard Marshal's brave fighting that can be compared to the bravery of his father, William Marshal, who had been a renowned statesman and feared warrior. Wendover goes on to to say:

His (Marshal's) enemies at length, not daring to approach him, killed the horse he rode with their lances; but the Marshal, who was well practiced in the French way of fighting, seized one of the knights who was attacking him by the feet and dragged him down to the ground, and then quickly mounting his adversary's horse, he renewed the battle. The knight Baldwin was so ashamed that the Marshal defended himself single-handed against so many of his enemies for such a time, that he made a desperate attack on him and seizing his helmet, tore it from his head with such violence, that blood gushed forth from his nostrils and his mouth; he then seized the Marshal's horse by the bridle and endeavoured to drag it with its rider towards the [Monmouth] castle.

It appears at this point, while Richard Marshal was still valiantly fighting off his attackers, a crossbowman discharged a bow, hitting Baldwin in the chest, which pierced his armour and his body. The knights trying to hold onto Richard Marshal then hurried to get Baldwin to safety, not knowing if he was mortally wounded.

He wasn't but was seriously wounded and he was carried back to Monmouth Castle. However, the Marshal's reinforcements had been sent for so the castle garrison fled back towards the castle. Many prisoners and horses were taken from both sides of the battle but worse was to come when the Castle Bridge, which went over the Monnow from the castle and onto Castle Field at the time, collapsed and many men and horses were drowned. Both Bassett and Siward made it back to Chepstow with Marshal and planned further ambushes. One of these was in Grosmont woods where, on 26 December 1233, John of Monmouth had planned on making a secret attack on the Marshal but was severely routed by Marshal's forces after Marshal had learned of the plan. According to the Oxford Dictionary of National Biography, John of Monmouth narrowly escaped being caught and the Flores Historiarum states that:

When therefore the enemy came to the place of the ambuscade, the Marshal and his army rushed on them amidst the din of horns and trumpets and taking them unawares, soon put them all to flight, and closely pursuing them, slew great numbers ... and John [of Monmouth] himself with much difficulty escaped by flight.

In April 1234, Richard Marshal was injured and captured while fighting on his lands in Ireland and died from his wounds. This bought the Marshal rebellion to an end and in May 1234, both Gilbert Bassett and Richard Siward were pardoned by the king and had

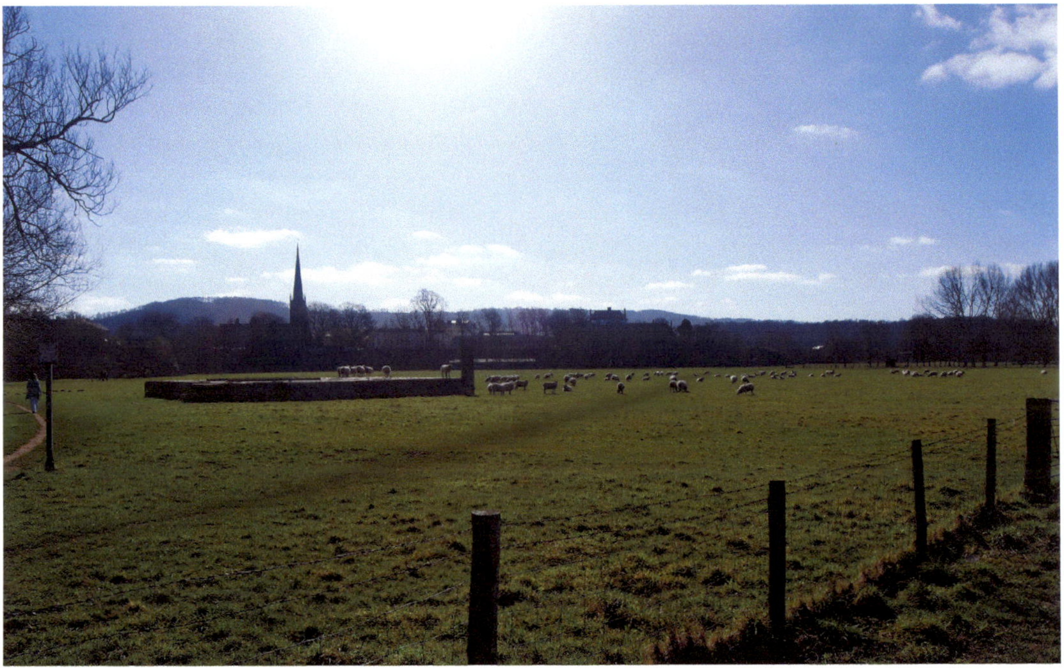

Vauxhall Fields, also known as a water meadow, looking towards Monmouth town. (Image courtesy of Anthony Cope under Creative Commons 3.0)

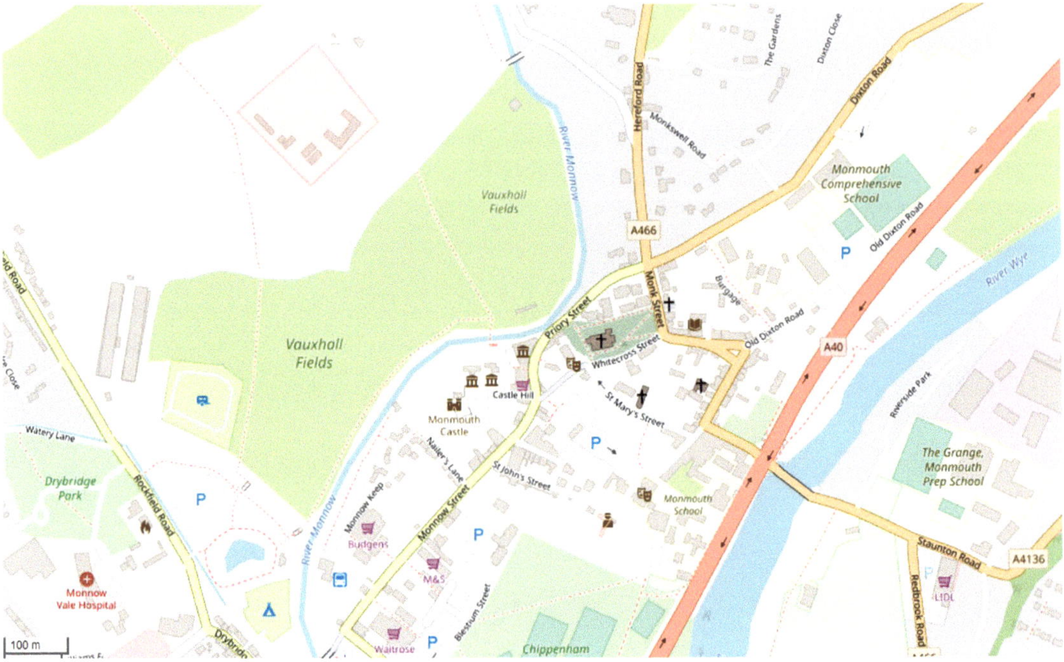

Map showing location of Vauxhall Fields today. (OpenStreetMap Contributors available under Open Database Licence)

their lands restored. Bassett died in 1241 and his sister/cousin, Phillippa divorced her husband, Richard Siward, in 1242, which is unusual for this era but could possibly be due to the fact she may have been under duress when she married him. Siward retired to lands in Scotland and died from a stroke in 1248. This was the same year that John of Monmouth died and Monmouth Castle passed to his son, John.

GGAT report the most probable site of the battle was Castle Field, now known as Vauxhall Fields. It was the Battle of Monmouth that destroyed the Grace Dieu Abbey, at the instigation of Richard Marshal's Welsh allies, as well as St Thomas' being set alight and the destruction of the original wooden bridge we know as Monnow Bridge. This wasn't rebuilt in stone until around 1272, although could have possibly been as early as 1262 according to Rowland's book *Monnow Bridge and Gate.*

Archenfield

Once known as Ariconium, the area we now know as southern Herefordshire was once a road station mentioned in the Antoine Itineraries, the source document that registers all the Roman roads and stations, with Ariconium being one of many place names within the British section called Iter Britanniarum. Although not a lot else is known about it, the document proves to be a valuable resource for Roman place names.

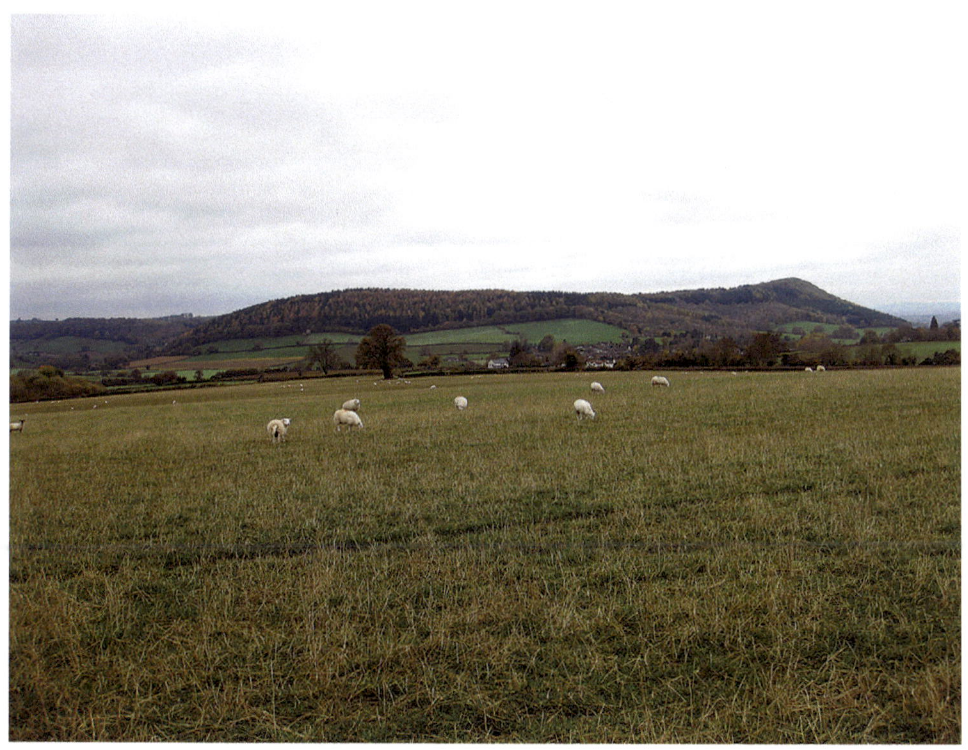

In the parish of Bury Hill, looking towards Weston-under-Penyard, once the ironworking Roman town of Ariconium, then known as the Welsh commote of Erging, to become Archenfield. (Image courtesy of Pauline E under Creative Commons 2.0)

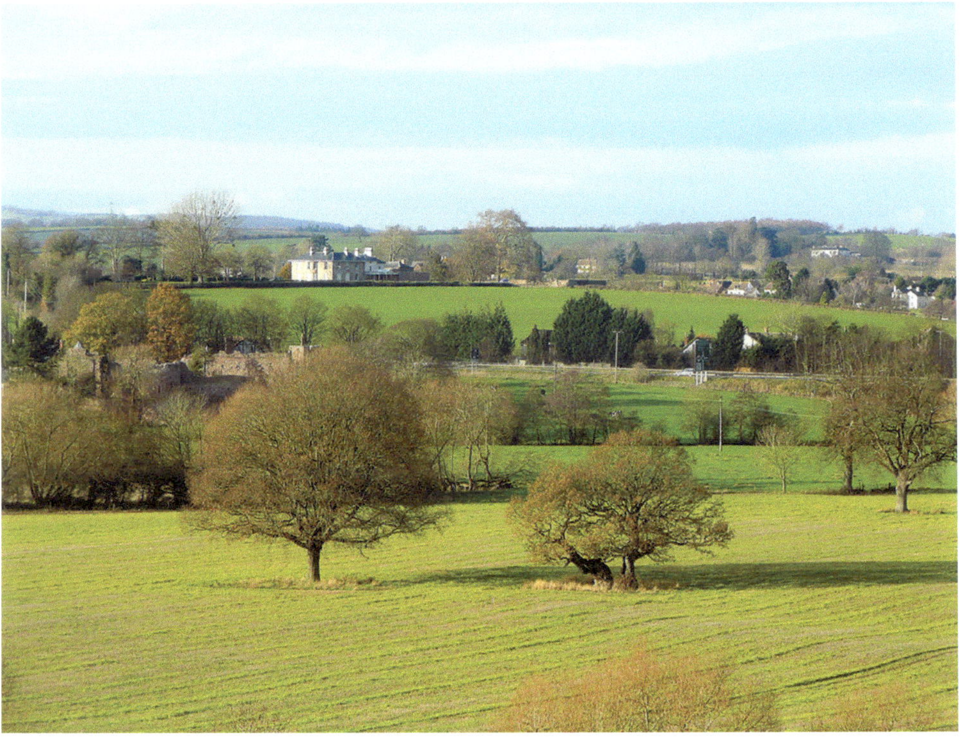

Part of the area known as Archenfield. (Image courtesy of Jonathan Billinger under Creative Commons 2.0)

Ariconium is believed to be in the area around Bury Hill, near the village of Weston-under-Penyard, and evidence of forges and ironworkings have been found. There may have been inhabitants that possibly predate the Romans. The area would have been very industrial in its time but it appears to have been abandoned after AD 360 and quite suddenly, which would tie in with the beginning of the Roman departure of its furthest conquered lands including Britainnia, after recall from Rome and the eventual collapse of the Roman Empire around AD 410. It was a time of unrest for the Empire, as documented by a Roman soldier and historian Ammianus Marcellinus: '...at length the reigns of terror instituted by successive emperors and by the deplorable crew of secret police, spies and informers who surrounded them.'

Writing in 1854, Thomas Wright in *The Wanderings of an Antiquary: Chiefly Upon the Traces of the Romans in Britain* wrote about discussing Ariconium with the local population in Bury Hill:

Fifteen centuries ago this slightly elevated ground was covered with a flourishing town, from which several roads branched off to different parts of the country. The fields and hedgerows which have taken the place occupied once by busy streets and joyous hearths have nothing in appearance to distinguish them from those of the country around; yet the peasantry still look with a certain degree of reverence on the spot, and they can tell you mysterious stories of the vengeance which fell upon the ancient town and its inhabitants. If you enter the first cottage that presents itself in the village of Weston and ask the inmates to the way to the old town, they will reply without hesitation, "What sir, the town that was beaten down and all the people killed?" and they will at once point you to the site and tell you that the field sloping down to the brook is called Killington meadow was so named because the blood ran down there from the people that were *killed...*

Flourishing anecdotal writing maybe but the telling of stories being handed down was once the only way to communicate ancient knowledge.

The most Romanized part of Wales had been the south-eastern corner and when the Roman Empire fell and withdrew from Britain in around AD 410, this area fell into three kingdoms from an eclectic mix of the old tribal Silure traditions and Roman settlements. These three areas were Gwent (after the fall of Caerwent, *c.* AD 500), Erging and Glywysing (Glamorgan). Each had its own royal house. The kings of Erging were most powerful in the era AD 500–600 but eventually merged by royal marriage and war, the records showing that Glamorgan had assimilated both Gwent and Erging by AD 600, thus having control over large areas of south-eastern Wales.

The working settlement that had been Aricronium became Caer Aricon (now known as Weston-under-Penyard); the Welsh translation was *Erging/Ergying* and the English translation became Archenfield.

The National Library of Wales holds an article entitled *The Chronology in the Book of Llan Dav 500–900.* It is an attempt to study the chronology of the kingdoms and kings of south-east Wales and within the diocese (ecclesiastical administrative district) that once included the Wye Valley. *The Book of Llan Dav/Llandaff,* as we have seen, is the register of the church of the early history of the diocese. The article notes how in the early to mid-eighth century, a king of Erging had the frontier boundaries restored after a period of warfare, which had also depopulated the region. This was the time of King Aethelbald of Mercia and the frontier boundaries were most probably ravaged over time by the incursion of the Saxons. It was conquered by the Anglo-Saxons by the ninth century and in the tenth century (some sources say eleventh century) a primary source document, the Ordinance Concerning the Dunsæte, tells us how Archenfield was unusual in having a mixed Anglo-Welsh community of long standing cooperation:

A region where two peoples and two cultures came together relatively equitably for a long period of time and out of that region's role as a nexus [connection] between Welsh and Mercian cultures something new and distinctive occurred. *Writing the Welsh Borderlands in Anglo-Saxon England* (Brady, 2017)

Recent historians have highlighted that the written words of 'conquest' and 'ravages' should be more akin to the reality of a piecemeal migration of Anglo-Saxons. The main issue within the area around the Wye appears to have been cattle stealing and the agreement was drawn up to outline specific trade procedures. What made the Ordinance

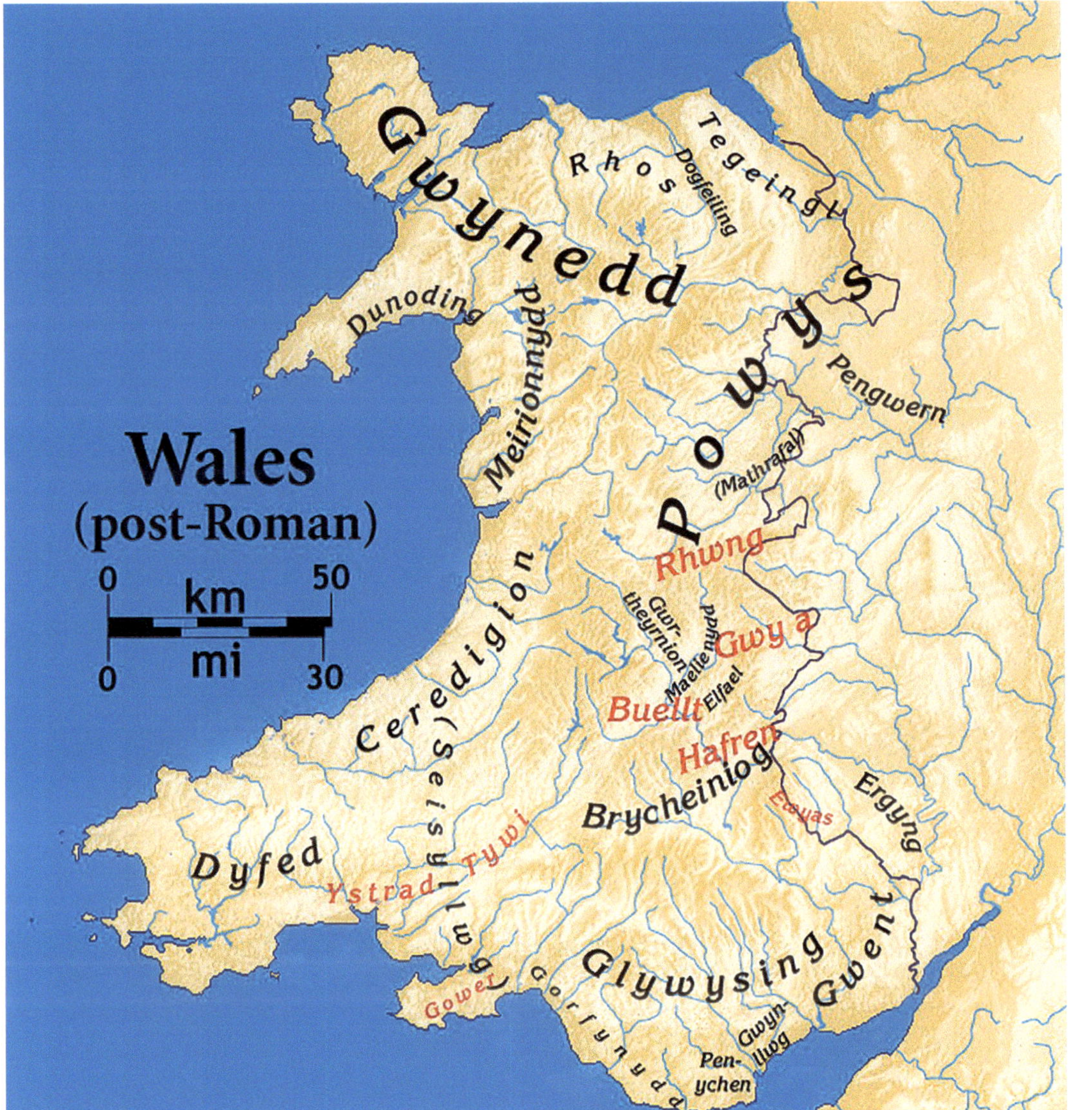

Concerning the Dunsæte different to other Anglo-Saxon charters is that the agreement was put in place among the Dunsæte by English and Welsh counsellors.

The 'Dunsæte' (meaning 'hill people') are thought to have inhabited the area from Monmouth to Hereford, thus early Monmouth inhabitants would have been enjoying the age-old traditions and devotion to the Celtic church that they had been enjoying when William FitzOsbern arrived in 1067. He was by then Earl of Hereford and easily overran the area of Archenfield. FitzOsbern and his successors manipulated this however, agreeing to let the people keep their traditions and Celtic customs without interference in return for military service. Kissack notes how the men of Archenfield were 'compelled to act as vanguard on the advance and rearguard on the withdrawal', vulnerable areas open to attack, but as well as being permitted to live within their old tribal ways, they had also had a reputation:

> In the Middle Ages, Giraldus Cambrensis, otherwise known as Gerald of Wales (1146–1223), reports Archenfielders were impetuous and volatile, lacking in loyalties and ferocious fighters. This reputation made the Archenfielders rather attractive to the kings of England who commissioned them as mercenaries in their armies. In turn, these Archfielders were given special privileges and referred to as the 'kings-men'. The Ross Library Group

Kissack, writing in his book *Medieval Monmouth*, notes how the traditions of the people of Archenfield, which were prevalent in Monmouth, were given a section in the Domesday Book, some of which is written below, and gives us an idea of the 'traditions' that were allowed in Archenfield (adapted from Kissack's book):

> In Arcenefelde the king has three churches. The priests of these convey the messages of the king of Wales and eachof them sings two masses for this king each week. When any of these dies the king has 20s from him by custom.
>
> If one of the Welshmen steals a man or woman, horse, ox or cow, upon conviction thereof, he first restores the stolen goods, and then gives 20s for the offence. For a stolen sheep, however or a bundle of sheaves he pays 2s fine.
>
> If anyone kills one of the kings-men and commits heinfare he gives the king 20s. in payment for the man and 100s for the offence. If he kills a thane's man he gives 10s for the dead man's lord.
>
> If so be that a Welshman shall kill a Welshman the relatives of the slain meet together and plunder the slayer and his kin, and burn their houses until on the morrow at about noon the corpse of the dead man is buried. Of this plunder the king has a third part, but they have all the rest without interference.
>
> And moreover he who shall have a set a house on fire and been accused thereof, defends himself by 40 men and if he shall be unable to do so he shall pay 20s to the king … these are the customs of the Welsh in the time of King Edward in Arcenefelde.

This state of affairs stayed in situ until the Laws of Wales Act 1536 under Henry VIII when the politics, administrative and law anomalies were abolished and the Marcher lands ceased to exist in any formal arrangement. Five new shires were created: Denbigh, Montgomery, Radnor, Brecon and Monmouth, with the eastern lordships annexed to Shropshire and Herefordshire. Archenfield came under Herefordshire but remained Welsh speaking until around the seventeenth century. According to John Davies in his *History of Wales,* the new shires now became the border between England and Wales and still exist today, breaking tradition by not following Offa's Dyke nor the eastern boundaries of the Welsh dioceses.

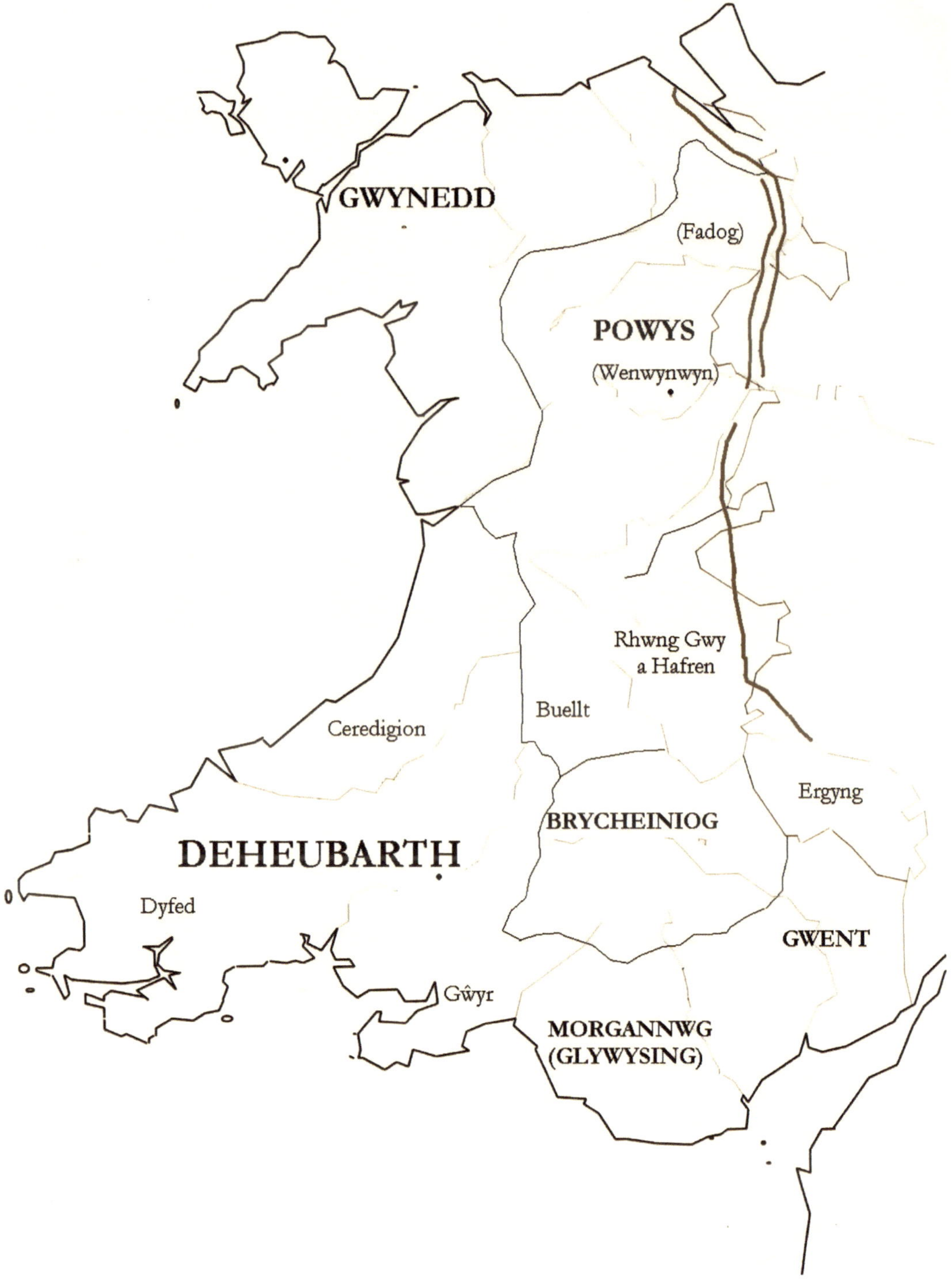

Medieval map of Wales. Note the presence of Erging/Ergyng.

5. Crime and Punishment

One of Monmouth's many outstanding buildings has to be the Shire Hall. Built in 1724 on the site of an older building from 1571, which, in turn, had replaced a *c.* 1536 court building, it was the centre for assize courts and quarter sessions for Monmouthshire until 1997. These were sessional hearings for both crime and civic cases overseen by judges who travelled the 'circuits' hearing trials across England and Wales.

However, assizes had originally been heard in the Great Hall at Monmouth Castle, built by a son of Henry III, Edmund Crouchback, 1st Earl of Lancaster. In 1673 – and after the damage wrought on Monmouth Castle by Cromwell's troops – Great Castle House was built on the site of what had been the Great Tower, using bricks from this and possibly the gatehouse. Courts were heard here until 1724 when sessions moved to the Shire Hall. In 1875, the Grade I listed Great Castle House became the home of Royal Monmouth Royal Engineers (RMRE) and it is still their headquarters today as well as the regimental museum. This army unit have unbroken service since 1539. After their initial muster as a militia, they became *posse comitatus,* a group of people mobilised by authority – usually the sheriff – to defend their county, and the term was shortened to posse from the late seventeenth century.

The Chartist Movement lasted from 1838–1857 and had strongholds in northern England, East Midlands as well as the South Wales valleys and was an early form of trade union.

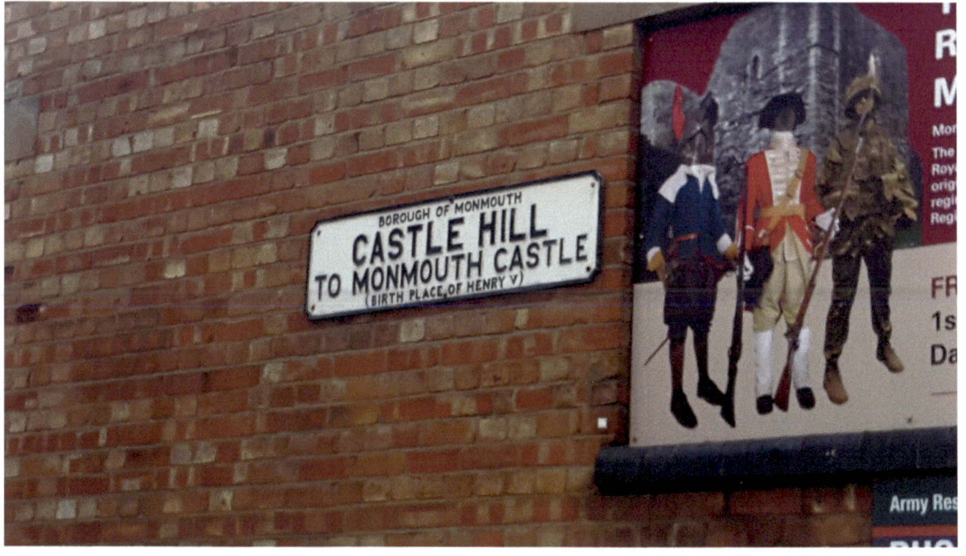

Road sign on the road leading up to the remains of Monmouth Castle and the gatehouse.

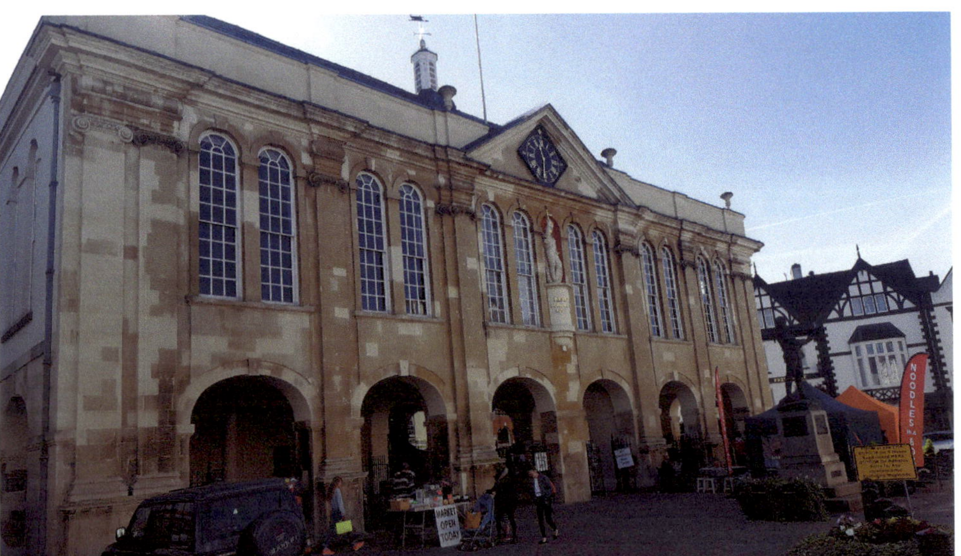

It is common knowledge that the famous trial of the leaders of the Chartist movement was heard here, at the Shire Hall. All three men were deported from Chepstow Port.

In 1832 the Reform Act allowed only those who held property would be able to vote, thus most voters were from the middle and upper classes. Then in 1834, the Poor Law forbid any working men from claiming Outdoor Relief, thus forcing working families into workhouses and being separated once inside. The Industrial Revolution had produced a mass workforce over the years and Chartists believed in a fairer democratic system and better living conditions for the working classes. These three men who sailed from Chepstow Port, stood up and spoke out for the Chartist beliefs; leading men to Newport on an uprising that was bloody and violent and unfortunately ended in the Chartist defeat at this point. However, John Frost, William Jones and Zephaniah Williams were convicted of High Treason in November 1839 at the Shire Hall in Monmouth and sentenced to be hanged, drawn and quartered, a punishment first recorded in the thirteenth century and abolished in 1870. This was commuted to transportation for life and in 1856, all were given unconditional pardons. John Frost returned to Bristol to live with his daughter and died in 1877 aged ninety-three and is buried in Bristol. William Jones, a watchmaker, remained in Australia as a watchmaker, dying in poverty in 1873 and Zephaniah Williams, a coal miner, discovered coal on Tasmania and founded the Tasmanian coal trade, dying in 1874 a wealthy man. *Secret Chepstow* (Wyatt, 2018)

Crimes committed in all towns within Monmouthshire (Chepstow, Usk, Raglan, Caldicot etc.) were heard at Shire Hall in Monmouth. The following picture shows a cutting from *The Cambrian*, 18 April 1835, describing the scene of the hanging of Edward Morgan at Monmouth Gaol, who was found guilty of murder during a riot when a gun went off 'accidentally'. He had a nature of good repute but, according to the paper, 'about four years ago had discontinued this course, sin gained an ascendency in his mind and he

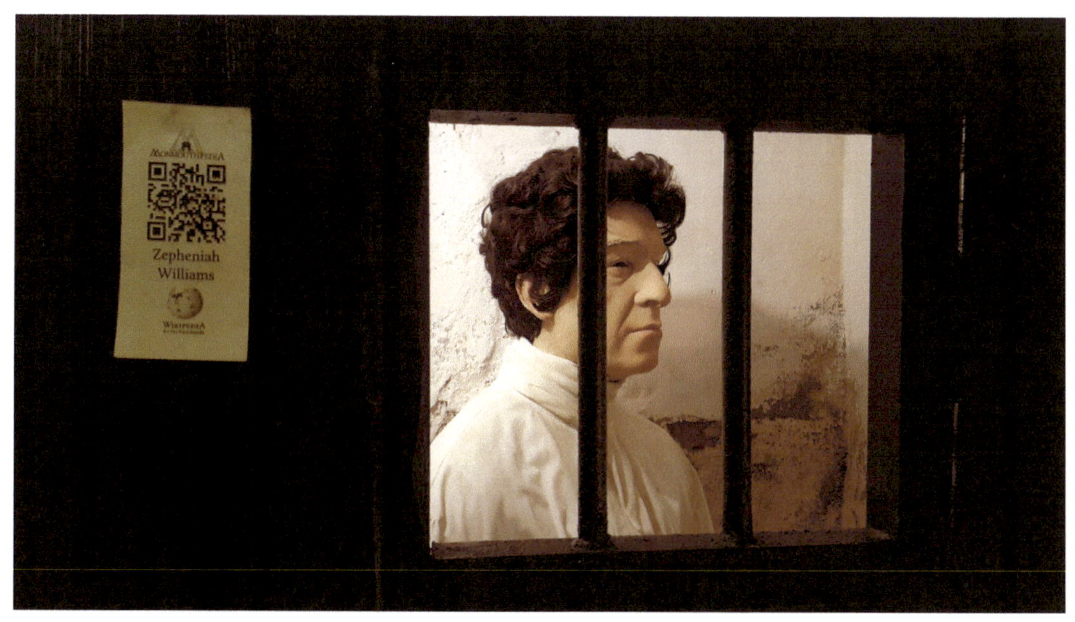

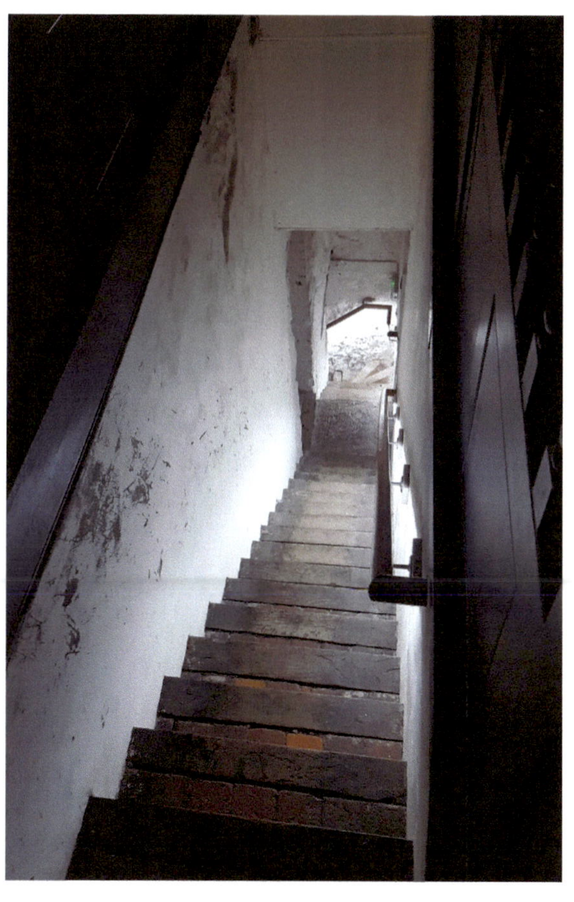

Above: In the holding cells below the courtrooms in Shire Hall. Here we see Zepheniah Williams awaiting his trial. Note the link to 'Monmouthpedia' on the left.

Left: Staircase down to the holding cells from Court No. 1, Shire Hall.

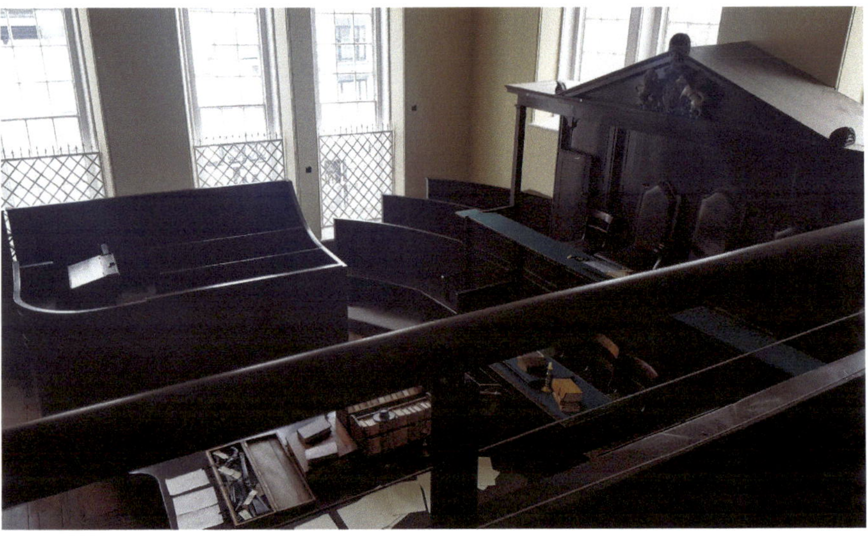

Many trials have taken place in Shire Hall and this picture shows Court No. 1 taken from the public gallery and looking to the judge's bench.

The prison bell began to toll at a quarter past twelve, and shortly after we saw the wretched man coming forth from his cell, in a deplorable state of physical prostration; he tottered slowly on, supported by two officers; his face as pale as if he had already been a tenant of the grave, gazing wildly and vacantly on all around; groaning most piteously, and sobbing broken and incoherent ejaculations for divine mercy. Oh! that his associates in crime had witnessed the heart-rending scene of those bitter and agonising moments. Oh! that the malefactors, whose nocturnal depredations have disgraced the character of their hitherto peaceful county, had the sad lesson of his haggard features and streaming eyes, pourtraying penitence and remorse, which were, alas! too late for mercy in this world. Oh! that they had heard his piteous lamentations for sinful deeds, and we know not of what materials the hearts of those combinators are formed, if they would not have returned to their homes better men; if they would not have seen, with the most hearty resolves of amendment, the madness and misery of illegal combinations, which will not, and cannot, come to good, but which, on the contrary, lead to beggary, imprisonment, and death!—in a word, if they would not abandon their criminal career—" cease to do evil, and learn to do well."

On arriving at the room leading to the platform, the poor fellow addressed the High Sheriff (who evinced feelings honourable to our nature, in the discharge of his unpleasant duties) for permission to pray a few minutes: this was, of course, readily granted, and in the most consoling terms. His prayers were Welsh, and in a singing strain, and offered with fervour; they were to the following purport:—" O Lord, receive my soul, though of one who has forgotten thy ways. I am a sinner, but thou art merciful; Jesus

The Cambrian, 18 April 1835.

hearkened to evil-doers'. Unfortunately for Edward, his hangman would have been the one with a notorious reputation – Mr William Calcraft, who was hangman at Monmouth Gaol between 1829 and 1874. He used a short piece of rope, which led to a slower, more strangulated death. The paper also describes the scene as awful and revolting and thankfully of rare occurrence at Monmouth Gaol. Two fellow convicts were reprieved but Edward Morgan was not so fortunate and left a pregnant wife and three young children.

DID YOU KNOW?
Kelly's Directory, a Victorian version of Yellow Pages, was a trade directory with copies still preserved and is now an important historical primary research source.

On Thursday 21 February 1895, *The Evening Express* ran an article describing a case heard at the courts of Monmouth Assizes:

Judge Grantham orders the 'cat' for two prisoners. Resuming the trials of prisoners at Monmouth Assizes on Thursday, awarded an administration of the dreaded 'cat' in two cases of robbery at Newport. The first case, John Barrett, aged 24, was sentenced to six months imprisonment and 15 lashes of the 'cat'. Charles Tom Golledge, who was jointly charged, was acquitted. In the second case, in which Andrew Murray and Mary Heal were convicted, the man was sentenced to six months imprisonment and twenty lashes of the 'cat' and the woman was sent penal servitude for three years.

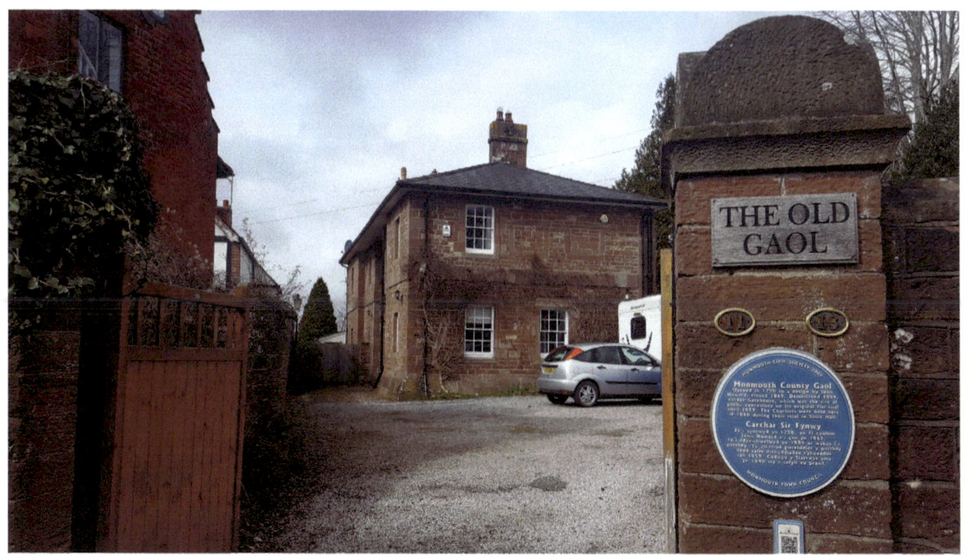

Remains of Monmouth Old Gaol with the only remaining building left, which is now a private residence.

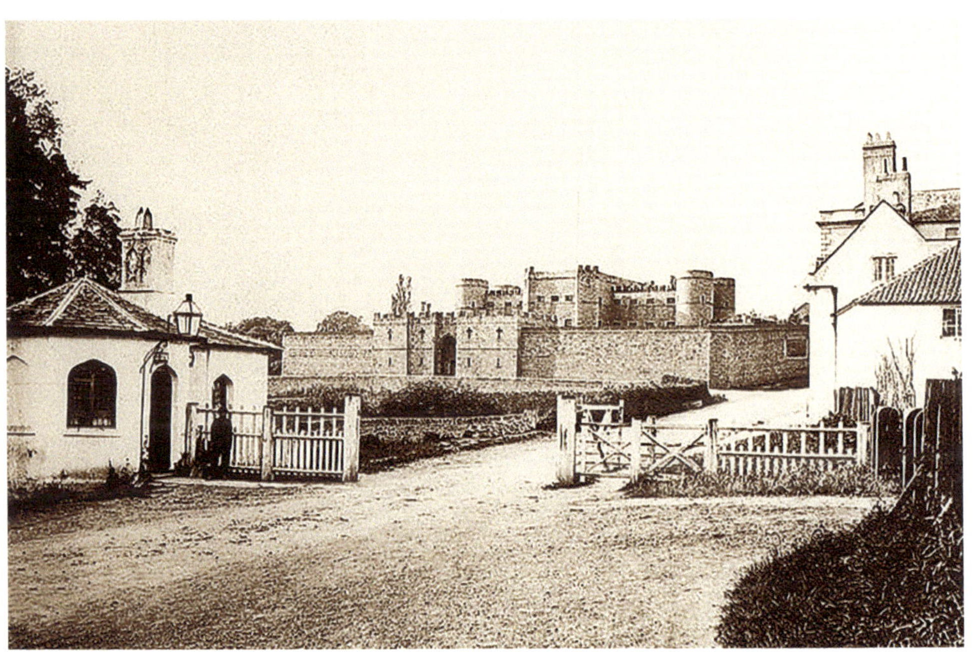

Above: Monmouth Gaol, *c.* 1820. The toll house on the left still survives today on the Hereford Road.

Right: Doorway to the tower stairway in the thirteenth-century Monnow Bridge Gate. The door, however, is of nineteenth-century materials and design. This Scheduled Monument also served as the town lock-up in its history.

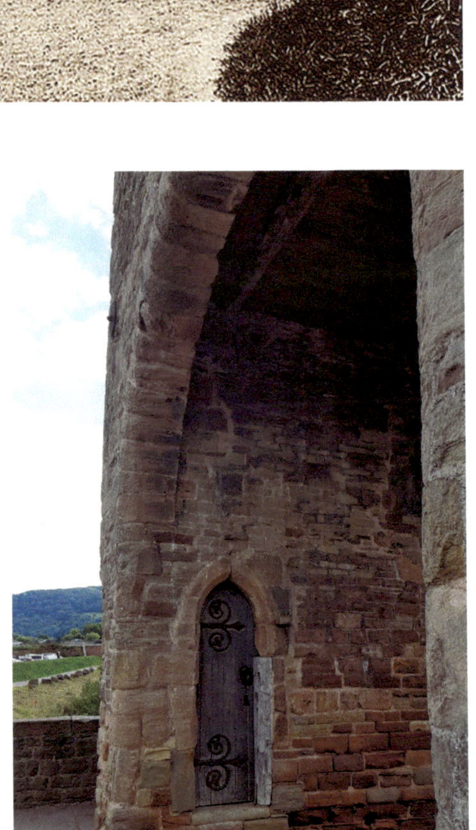

Monmouth had its fair share of deterrants over the course of its history: gallows on surrounding hills, stocks, whipping post and pillory in the Market Square, an old gaol in the Monnow Bridge Gatehouse and the new County Gaol.

Monmouth Gaol was built in 1790, with some alterations in 1820. In 1869, Monmouth Gaol was closed down and demolished in 1884, leaving only the gatehouse remaining with its original flat roof where the public executions took place. Inmates moved to the new gaol in Usk, where today's prison still survives. The old gaol is a Grade II listed building and is on the A466 road out of Monmouth to Hereford, an old toll road.

Monmouth Workhouse and Hospital

Many cases heard by the Monmouth magistrates related to disturbances from the Monmouth workhouse, mainly involving women. In *Monmouth: the Making of a County Town,* Kissack notes that there were twenty-four cases heard between 1853 and 1856, only three of which concerned men. Out of the twenty-one women, thirteen were sent to Monmouth Gaol.

Monmouth workhouse was, like many others across the kingdom, run by the local parish, as per the Poor Act of 1552:

In 1388, the Statute of Cambridge (12, Rich.II, c.7) came into force, which enabled Justices of the Peace of a Hundred (a division of land within a shire) to have more power restricting the movements of servants, beggars and labourers – the 'sturdy beggars'. Servants and labourers needed permission to move outside their hundred or risk being

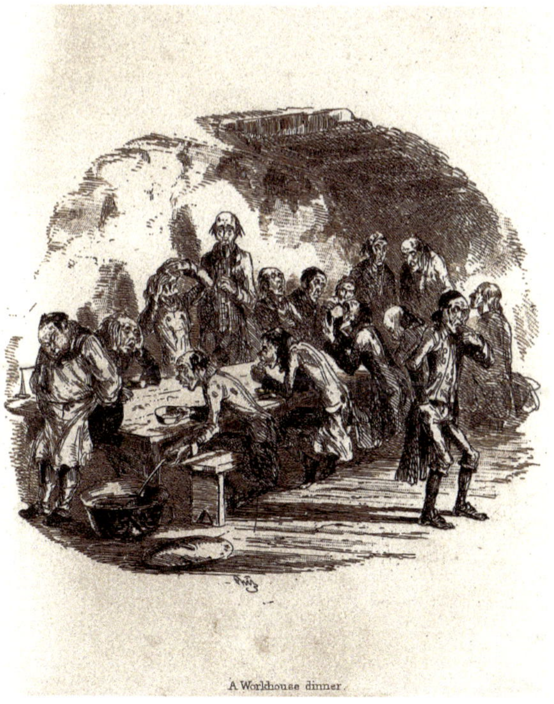

A caricature of a typical dinner scene in a workhouse in 1840. (Image courtesy of the Wellcome Library)

put in the stocks. This act also directed that the Hundred be responsible for its' own 'impotent poor' – the aged, infirm and incapable. In 1547, The Statute of Legal Settlement orders 'cottages' to be built for the impotent poor – possibly an early reference to an almshouse? – but also brands and enslaves those able bodies found begging. The Poor Act of 1552 declared that parishes collect alms to give out to the impotent beggars and keep registers of their poor, thus outlawing begging. The most comprehensive was the 1601 Act by Elizabeth I; this aimed at providing 'houses of dwelling' (early almshouses), providing apprenticeships for orphans and providing labour for the able-bodied poor.
Secret Chepstow (Wyatt, 2018)

Many paupers and beggars ended up in workhouses. The original parish workhouse was in Weirhead Street (which is now under the A40) and was the workhouse until 1860/61 when the new one was built near the gaol on the Hereford Road. It was also conveniently next to a cemetery!

DID YOU KNOW?
RMRE became an engineer unit in the nineteenth century and today are the most senior regiment within the British Territorial Army as well as the sole unit bearing the distinction of having two 'Royals' in their name.

Reporting on the state of Monmouth parish workhouse in 1797, Sir Frederick Eden in his *State of the Poor* notes a positive picture:

The poor are partly maintained in a work-house and partly at home; there are 24 persons at present in the work-house; of which 3 are children under 7 years of age; 12 between 7 and 30; and 9 between 30 and 79. They are chiefly employed in manufacturing linen and woollen cloths for the house. The house is convenient, and well aired, and appears to be kept very clean; the beds, which are good are furnished with coarse sheets: there are no blankets at present, but some are preparing against next winter. 45 out-pensioners receive, at present, £3 18*s* 3*d* a week; 4 or 5 receive occasional relief ... Several people belonging to the parish are employed in fisheries on the River Wye on which Monmouth is situated, and in navigating barges to and from this place.

Eden also noted of Monmouth that: 'In this town there are 20 alms-house; 10 for men and 10 for women, each of whom receives 3s 6d a week and 15s a year for coal; and 1 suit of cloaths every 2 years: 16*s* a week are paid for milita-men's families.'
Almshouses developed from the poor laws we saw earlier in this chapter. Agriculture had never recovered nationally from the Black Death – approximately a third of the nation was wiped out – and this saw a change from the old system

of the feudal manor to a system where peasants realised their worth. They were free and could move across the country to work for another lord, demanding higher wages, but the 1388 Act was aimed at restricting access for beggars and labourers, the able-bodied poor. The Black Death had ravished Monmouth and all around it in 1349, 1361 and 1369. Many people turned to superstition as death occurred just as highly in the clergy as it did the laity; many people flocked to churches for safety and they became centres of infection.

In his *Medieval Monmouth* book, Kissack notes:

By 1370, the minister's accounts show many entries dealing with the plague: increased rents, land in decay, payments in arrears, oxen in bad condition, mills let to farm, and land valued at over £12, 'in the hands of the lord through lack of tenants caused both by the First Pestilence as well as the pestilence happening there in 1369'.

The Monmouth Union took over from the parish to run the workhouse in 1836, which was an amalgamation of thirty-one parishes within Monmouthshire managed by a board of governors. However, this meant families were split up as the workhouse was no longer local and anyone could be living with you from areas such as Crick, Raglan, Skenfrith and English Bicknor to name just a few. Going into a workhouse was a last resort; life was tough and a typical day would begin at six a.m., breakfast at half past with work beginning at seven. Lunch would typically be between twelve

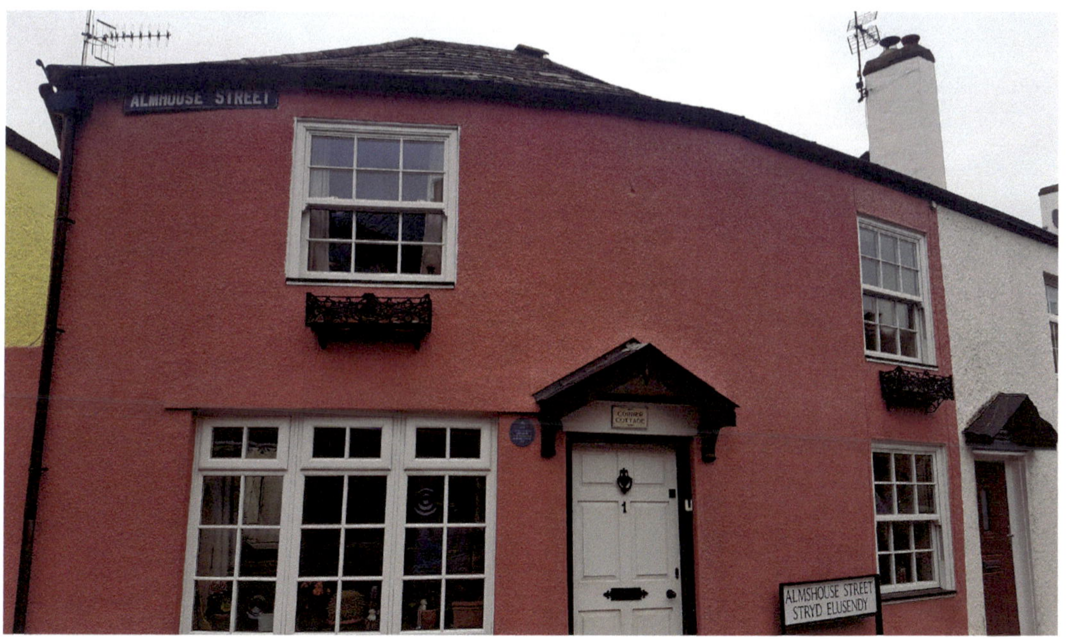

Beginning of the cottages in Almshouse Street (note the spelling error on the road sign on the cottage). These cottages were in the 1610 map of Monmouth by John Speed, shown earlier in the book.

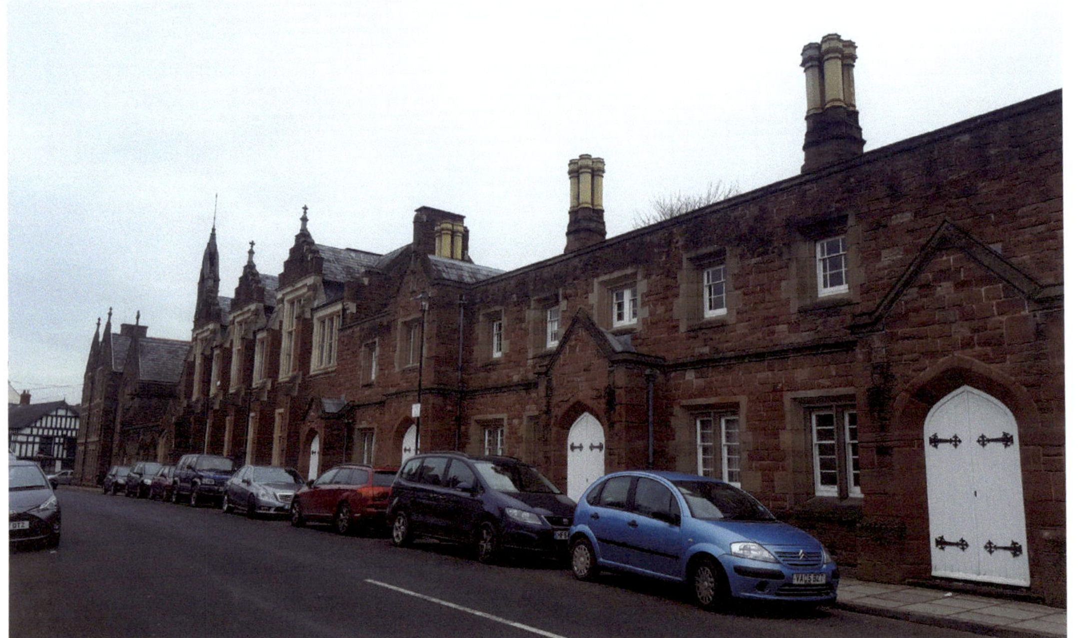

The original Jones Almshouses were built in 1614, which were rebuilt and incorporated into the Monmouth Boys' School above in 1842. William Jones was a wealthy haberdasher from Newland, Gloucestershire, who founded the group of Monmouth schools and his charity was managed by the Haberdasher Company (Guild) from 1613 until 2011. The charity is now managed by Bristol Charities.

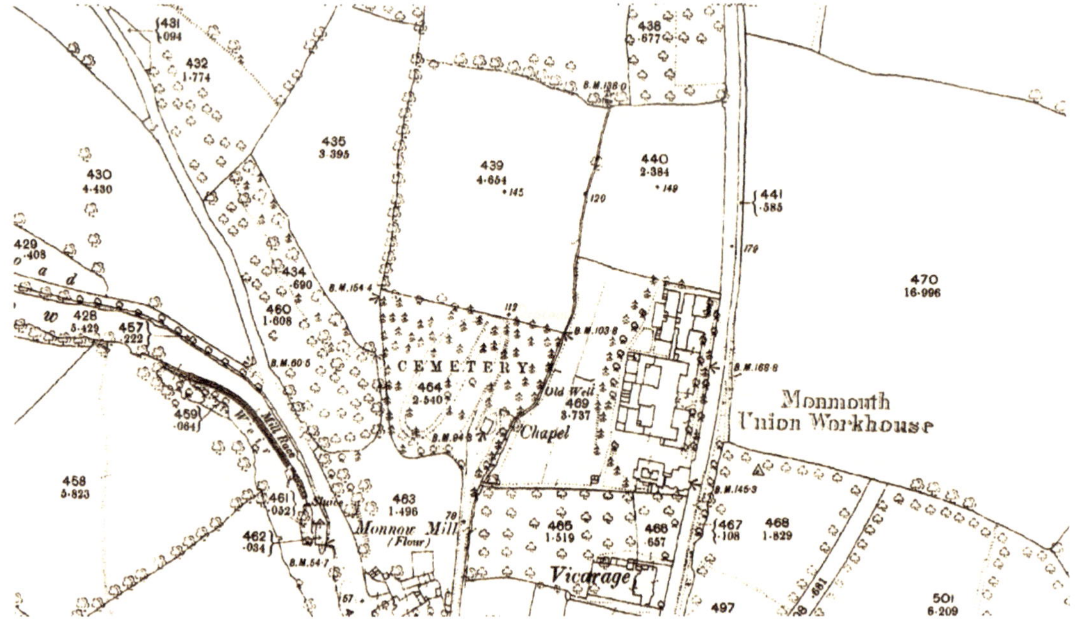

OS map of 1918 showing the location of Monmouth Workhouse and cemetery.

and one o'clock, with work finishing at six p.m., supper at seven and bed at eight p.m. Food was often varied to include meat a couple of times a week, broth, pudding and vegetables.

DID YOU KNOW?
The 'cat' was the original cat o' nine tails, a form of whip with several 'tails' intent on severe physical punishment and originating in the British Royal Navy and Army.

The 1861 census showed that Monmouth workhouse had eight inmates who were deemed long term, meaning they had been in there for over five years. They had variable descriptions attached to them such as idiot, old age, infirm, paralysis and rupture and weak of mind.

In 1870, the new building on the Hereford Road was constructed to cater for 200 inmates (as they were called then). It ceased to be a workhouse sometime after 1932 and the buildings that remain now form part of the Haberdasher's Monmouth School for Girls.

DID YOU KNOW?
According to the Welcome to Monmouth website, Monmouth was the first 'wikipedia town' in the world. This means applying QR codes to every piece of history possible – buildings, landscapes and so on – that can be accessed by a smartphone to relay any information in any language.

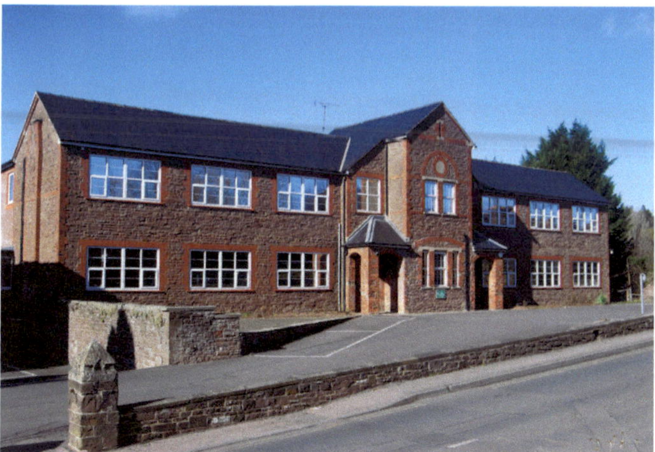

Originally the Workhouse Principal Building. (Image courtesy of Anthony Cope under Creative Commons 3.0)

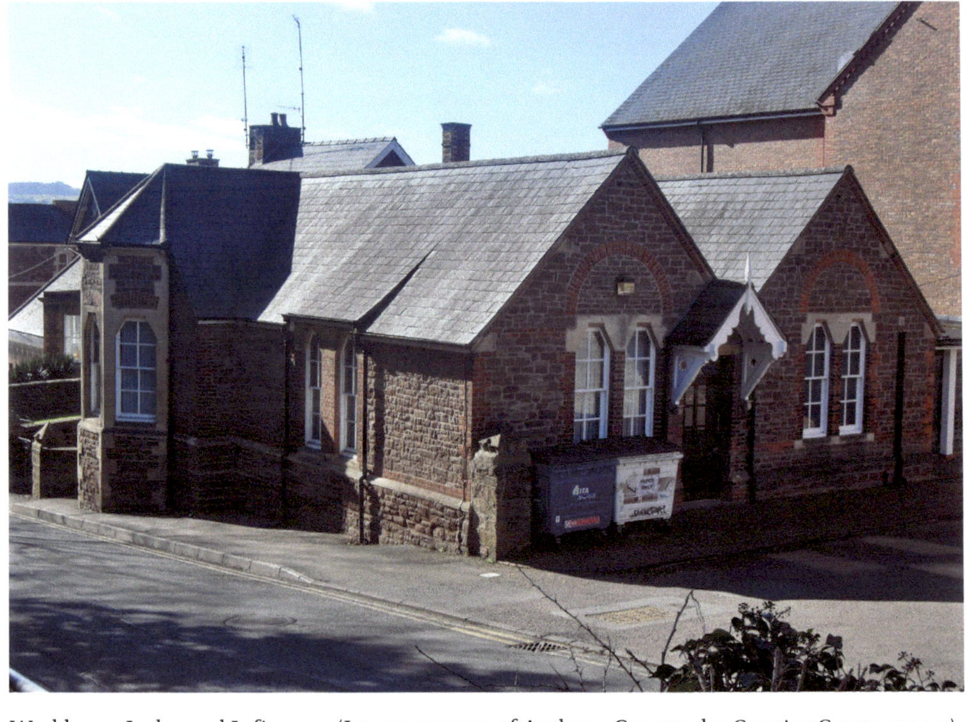

Workhouse Lodge and Infirmary. (Image courtesy of Anthony Cope under Creative Commons 3.0)

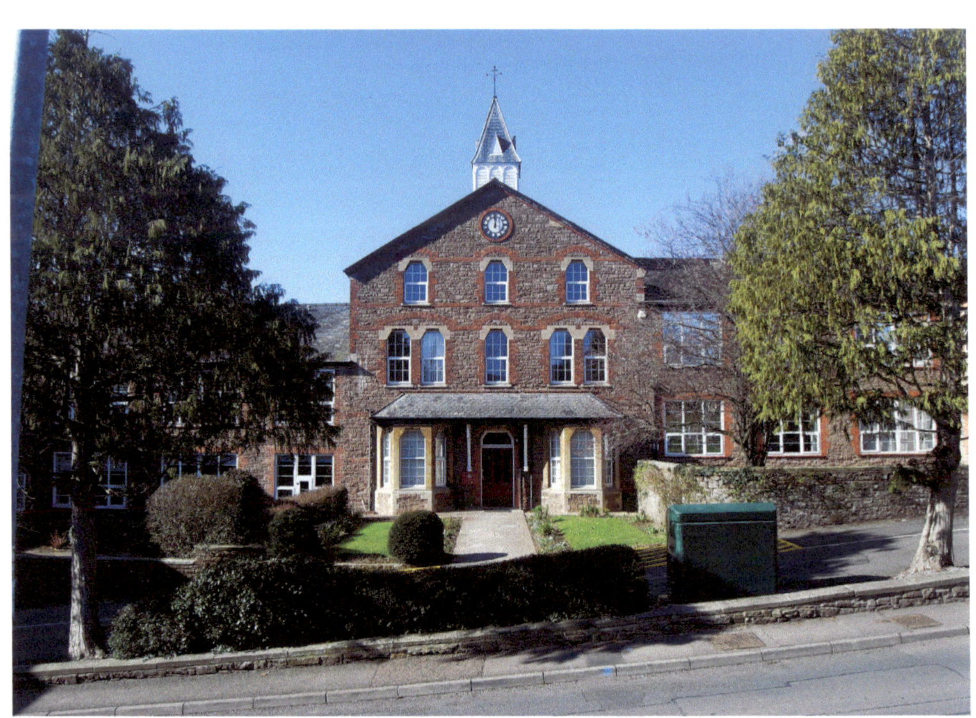

Workhouse receiving building. (Image courtesy of Anthony Cope under Creative Commons 3.0)

In 1895, Kelly's Directory described Monmouth workhouse as:

The old Workhouse, on the old Hereford Road, was erected in 1870–1, and consists of four blocks and buildings; viz., the lodge, the receiving building, a dining hall and chapel in the centre, & infirmary & is arranged to hold 204 inmates; the infirmary building is well appointed and has spacious airing grounds: in the rear of this building is a detached fabric for infectious cases: the whole of the buildings are of stone, enclosed with a low wall and palisading, and were erected at a cost of about £10,000 under the direction of Mr G. C. Haddon, architect, of Hereford and Great Malvern; F. Gunter, master; Rev W. M. Warlow, M.A chaplain; Thomas Gilbert Prosser, medical officer; Mrs Fanny Whittington, matron.

The medical officer, Thomas Gilbert Prosser (1856–1932), a native of Monmouth, was also the medical officer at Monmouth's hospital and dispensary, which was located in St James Square. Although living at home with his widowed mother and siblings in 1881, he was single and listed as a surgeon. He is listed as living in Chippenham House in 1891 but at St James House in 1901 and 1911. He was also a county magistrate and various newspaper reports of the time give him as surgeon to the gaol as well as the militia stationed at Great Castle House.

DID YOU KNOW?
James Paget (1814–99) was the son of a shipowner and brewer from Great Yarmouth. He discovered the condition now named after him – Paget's Disease – and worked sixteen to seventeen hours most days. He became Sir James Paget in 1875 for his work in surgery and pathology and has a hospital named after him in Great Yarmouth.

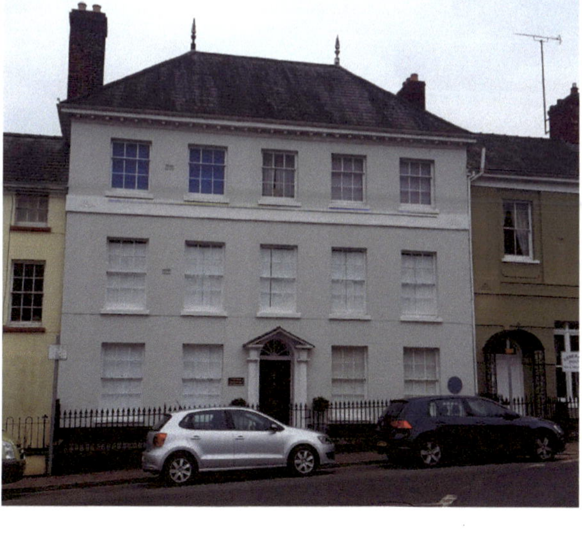

A Grade II listed building, the façade of this townhouse on St James Square dates from the mid-eighteenth century and became a dispensary in 1857. The building became a hospital and dispensary, opening with nine beds in 1868 and closed in 1903. Originally a burgage tenement in medieval times, archaeology has discovered a post-medieval pottery kiln at the rear of the property and St James Square is the area where finds relating to it being a lakeside Neolithic hunter-gatherer camp were found, as discussed in the first chapter.

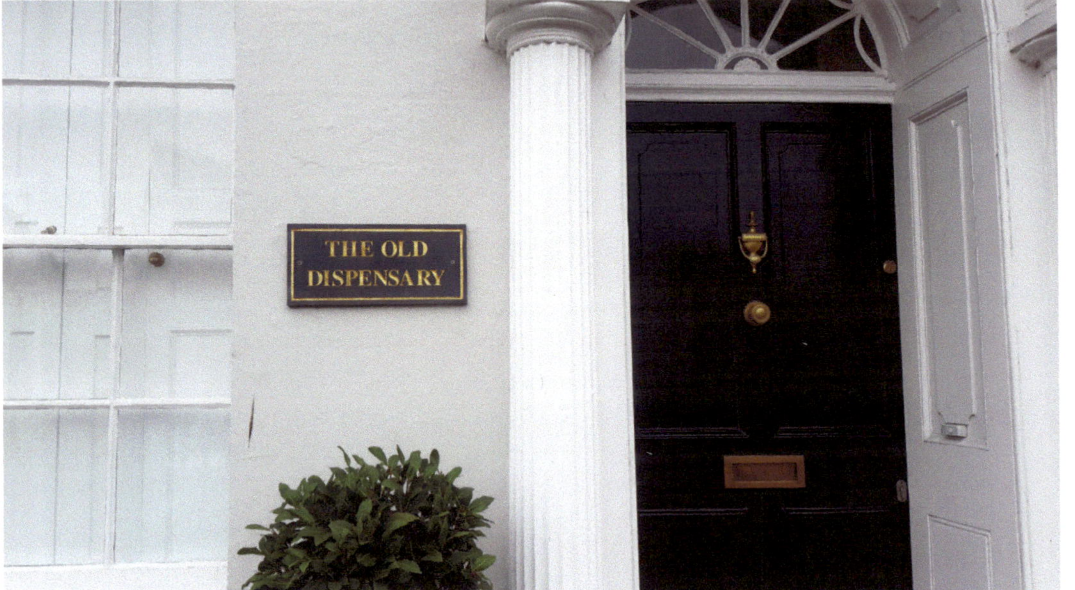

Above: In 1895, Kelly's Directory lists the staff working here as 'George Willis M.D, Thomas G Prosser & F. W. Brandram Jones M.D medical officers; William Dawe, dispenser and Wm. Hy. Nicholls L.D.S.R.C.S, dental surgeon'.

Right: Sir James Paget, eminent English surgeon and one of the world's first scientific pathologists, visited Monmouth Hospital and Dispensary in November 1873, according to Waugh in his *An Illustrated Handbook to Monmouth* (1875). Waugh goes on to say that 'The House is open to visitors and is well worthy of a visit, for Sir James Paget, who inspected it in November 1873, expressed his opinion that it was one of "the most convenient and best ventilated and arranged institutions he had ever seen."' (Image courtesy of the Wellcome Collection)

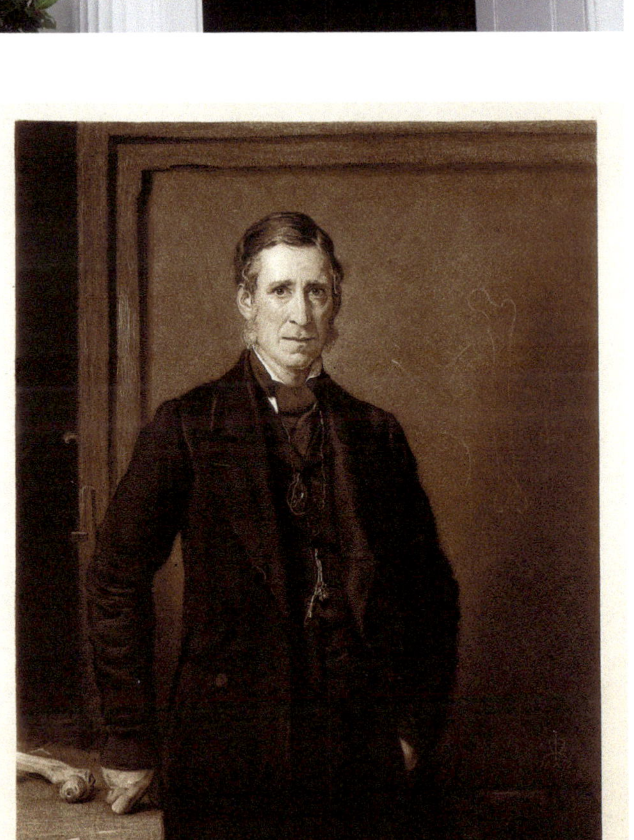

6. The Nelson Trail

The Kymin, approximately 1 mile east of Monmouth on the eastern side of the Wye and the National Trust property with strong ties to Lord Nelson, is thought to be on the site of a potential Iron Age hill fort; GGAT note how the site is identified on historic mapping but no determined remains have been found to date.

In 1803, Charles Heath, the local historian and printer, noted that the Welsh term was 'Cae-y-Maen', meaning 'large stone on a ledge/hill'. Further etymological investigations seem to agree with this: 'Cae', meaning 'fence' or 'hedge', is derived from the Celtic 'quay', and 'Maen' means 'ancient stone'. Kymin is actually the name of the hill. The National Trust property have owned the Round House since 1902 and building was instigated in 1794 by Philip Meakins Hardwick.

Hardwick prompted the building of the Round House, which sat on land owned by the Duke of Beaufort as a shelter to house the weekly meetings of the exclusive Picnic Club, a gathering of gentlemen in Monmouth. This gentlemen's club had been formed in the 1780s and became Monmouth Picnic Club and then the Kymin Club. There was a kitchen on the ground floor and a dining room above and was funded by the members including the Duke of Beaufort and eight members of parliament.

DID YOU KNOW?
Officers commissioned into the local Yeoman Cavalry/Provisional Forces had to be of an important local social standing but also wealthy, as most costs regarding the commission had to be met out of their own pockets.

Hardwick had been commissioned into the Yeoman Cavalry, the mounted contemporaries of the British Voluntary Corps, dedicated by an Act of George III in 1796 to 'raise a provisional force to be embodied in case of necessity for defence of these kingdoms'. The Act was a result of the fear of a possible invasion during the French Revolutionary Wars. Each county had a lord lieutenant who was the king's representative in such matters. In this case for Monmouth it was Henry Somerset, 5th Duke of Beaufort. The *London Gazette*, printed between 13 and 17 June 1796, announces that:

Commissions in the Provisional Cavalry, *of the County of* Monmouth, *signed by the Lord Lieutenant.*

Philip Meakins Hardwick, Esq; to be Captain Command Commandant. Dated April 26, 1797.

Hardwick therefore had links to the French wars so it is no surprise he built the Naval Temple at the Kymin in 1800, in celebration of the two-year anniversary of British victory in the Battle of the Nile and in recognition of Royal Navy Admirals. The temple was dedicated to the Duchess of Beaufort, daughter of one of the Admirals named on the Kymin Temple.

It is a well-known fact that Nelson visited Monmouth in 1802. During this summer, Nelson was to visit Milford in Pembrokeshire where his friend, Sir William Hamilton, had property and land. It is also known that Lady Emma Hamilton, wife of Sir William, was Nelson's mistress and had given birth to his daughter, Horatia, the year previous. Sources agree that the elderly Sir William, who was thirty-five years older than Emma, was tolerable of the affair and both he and Emma had a deep friendship. The ongoing and public affair didn't seem to interfere with the friendship and mutual respect between Nelson and Sir William either.

In his book *Monmouth: the Making of a County Town* Kissack says:

He [Nelson] was on his way, with Sir William and Lady Hamilton, and his brother and family, to visit Milford. It was a curious party. Lady Hamilton was thirty-seven, growing increasingly fat, but full of high spirits. Sir William was seventy-two and contented with a situation which gave him plenty of time for the study of antiquity. Nelson was

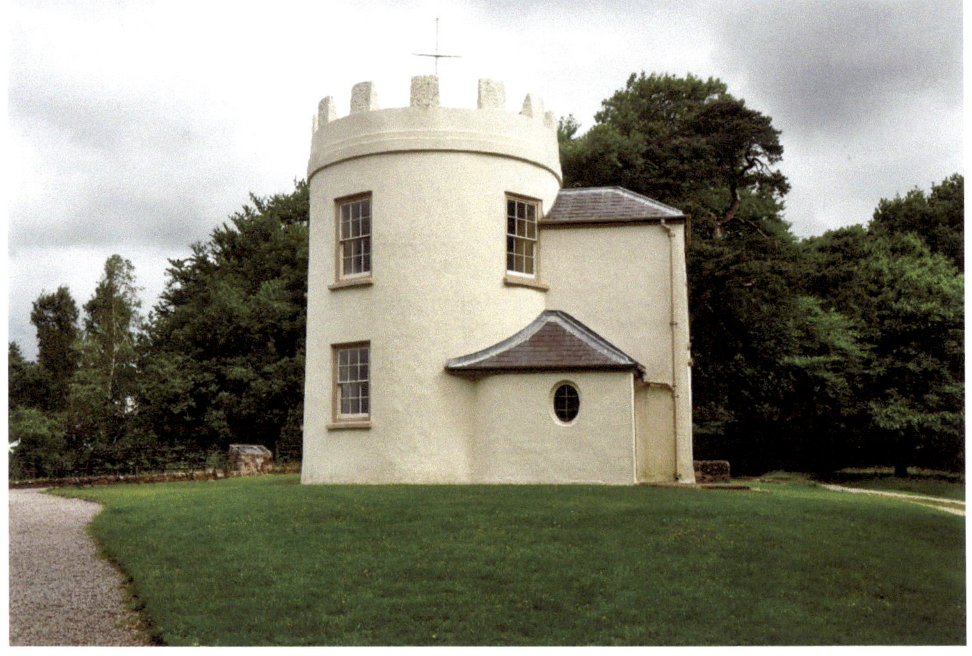

Round House on the Kymin. (Image courtesy of Nilfanion under Creative Commons 4.0)

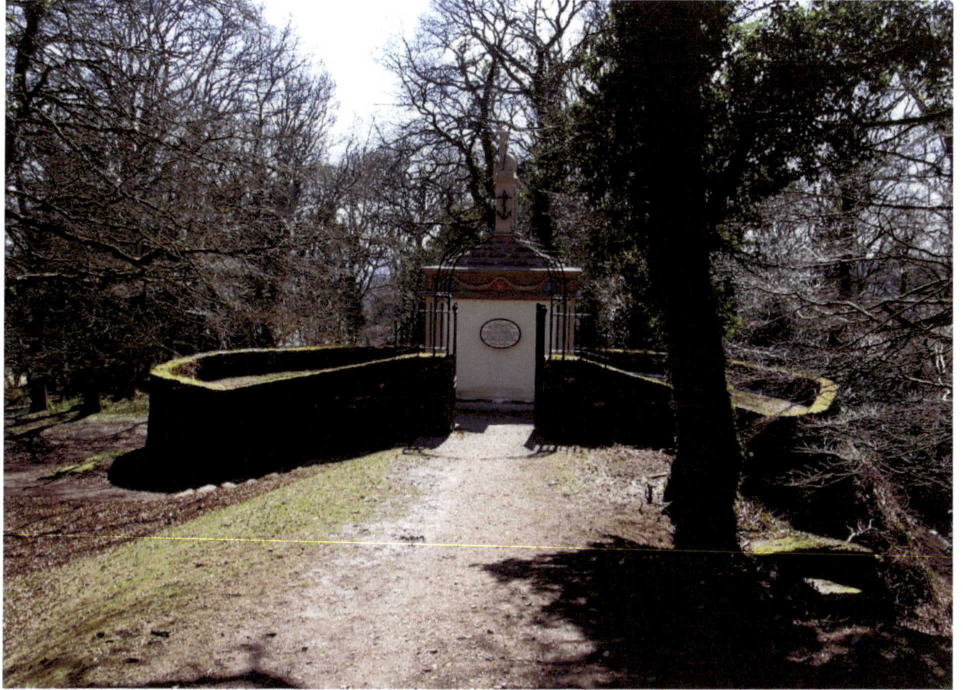

Approach to Naval Temple in the Kymin. (Image courtesy of Bill Boaden under Creative Commons 2.0)

forty-four, grey, lined, disappointed, with no right arm and a sightless right eye. He had wounds in the stomach, forehead and back, and was rarely out of pain ... he was parted from his wife to whom he was paying half his salary.

Due to price disputes with timber merchants, there was a desperate shortage of oak, leading to the crippling of dockyards and delays in shipbuilding, a major concern regarding the wars with France. HMS *Victory* had been built with 6,000 trees, 90 per cent of which were oak trees, supplied mainly by the Forest of Dean. Although the forest wasn't the only supplier to the docks and shipyards, Nelson also visited Chepstow and the timber merchants and settled the disputes. Nelson also visited the Forest of Dean and was disheartened to see no replanting of oaks:

It is known Nelson visited Wales – Pembrokeshire to be exact, where his friend, Sir William Hamilton, lived – and stopped off at the Forest of Dean in 1802 with regard to the timber supply for naval ships. Nelson was shocked at the amount of forest that had been cleared for charcoal furnaces for the Industrial Revolution and ordered a huge replanting of acorns for future oak trees. It was at this time that the naval dockyards were reportedly running low on timber for shipbuilding. Nelson's scathing report of the state of the Forest of Dean, where he discussed the mis-management of the area and put forward remedies, is now housed in the Nelson Museum in Monmouth. *Secret Chepstow* (Wyatt, 2018)

Thousands of acorns were planted and became known as the Trafalgar Oaks – 200 years later, two of these were used to refurbish HMS *Victory*.

In the 1980s excavations during the construction of a new vault beneath the Lloyds Bank building at No. 18 Monnow Street, Monmouth Archaeological Society discovered twelfth-century pottery remains and a diagonal ditch that carried on in nearby Nos 22–24 Monnow Street. Here they found evidence of the Roman invasion, Roman town, a post-Roman structure, the Norman defences and other medieval and post-medieval remains. Today, Lloyds Bank has a blue plaque marking the spot or thereabouts of the Roman fort and Norman defences, both diagonal to the current Monnow Street. The ditch below appears to run from the eleventh-century castle to Chippenham Fields next to the Nelson Garden.

DID YOU KNOW?
The Earldom of Nelson still exists, with Simon Nelson, a police officer, being the current 10th Earl. When Nelson died in 1805 at the Battle of Waterloo, he had no children other than his illegitimate daughter, Horatia, by his mistress Lady Emma Hamilton. Therefore, George III made his elder brother, Revd William Nelson, 1st Earl Nelson, giving him £90,000 to buy an estate (approx. £7.6 million today) and a pension of £5,000 per year (approx. £430,000 today).

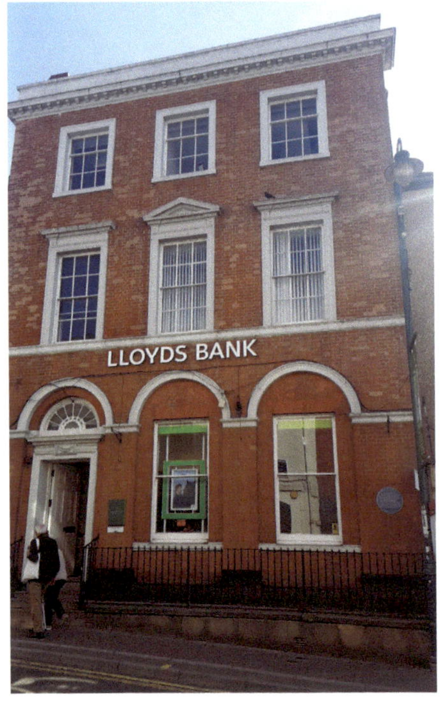

No. 18 Monnow Street, once a private residence and where Nelson took tea in the garden.

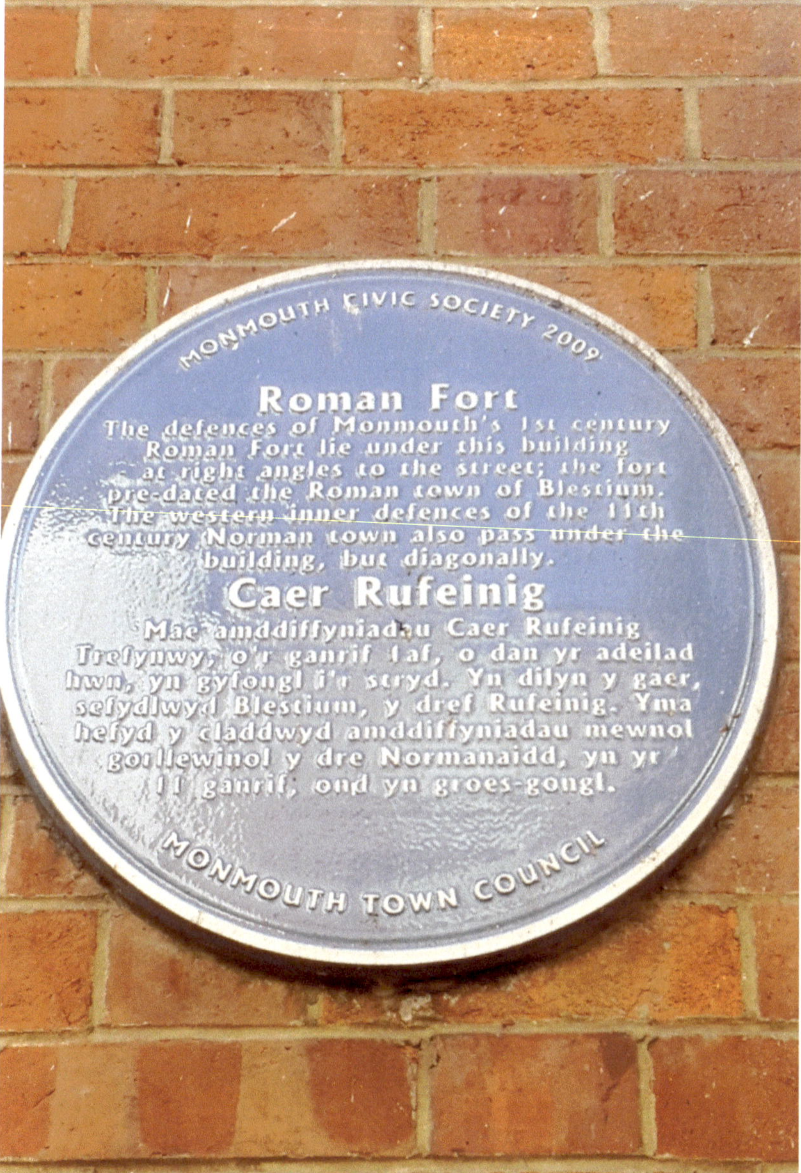

Blue plaque info on the front of Lloyds Bank, showing the history of the building. It is part of Monmouth's historically rich blue plaque trail.

The Nelson Garden was the garden of No. 18 Monnow Street. As well as Roman and Norman remains beneath, it had a seventeenth-century tennis court and an early eighteenth-century bowling green. The Georgian house belonged to Colonel Lindsay, the town clerk at the time of Nelson and the Hamilton's visit and they took tea in the garden in August 1802. The summer house they sat in was rebuilt in 1840 as a pavilion, but kept the original seat that Nelson sat on. All garden structures are now Grade II listed, and the Nelson Garden Preservation Trust Committee continues to manage the garden on behalf of Lloyds TSB.

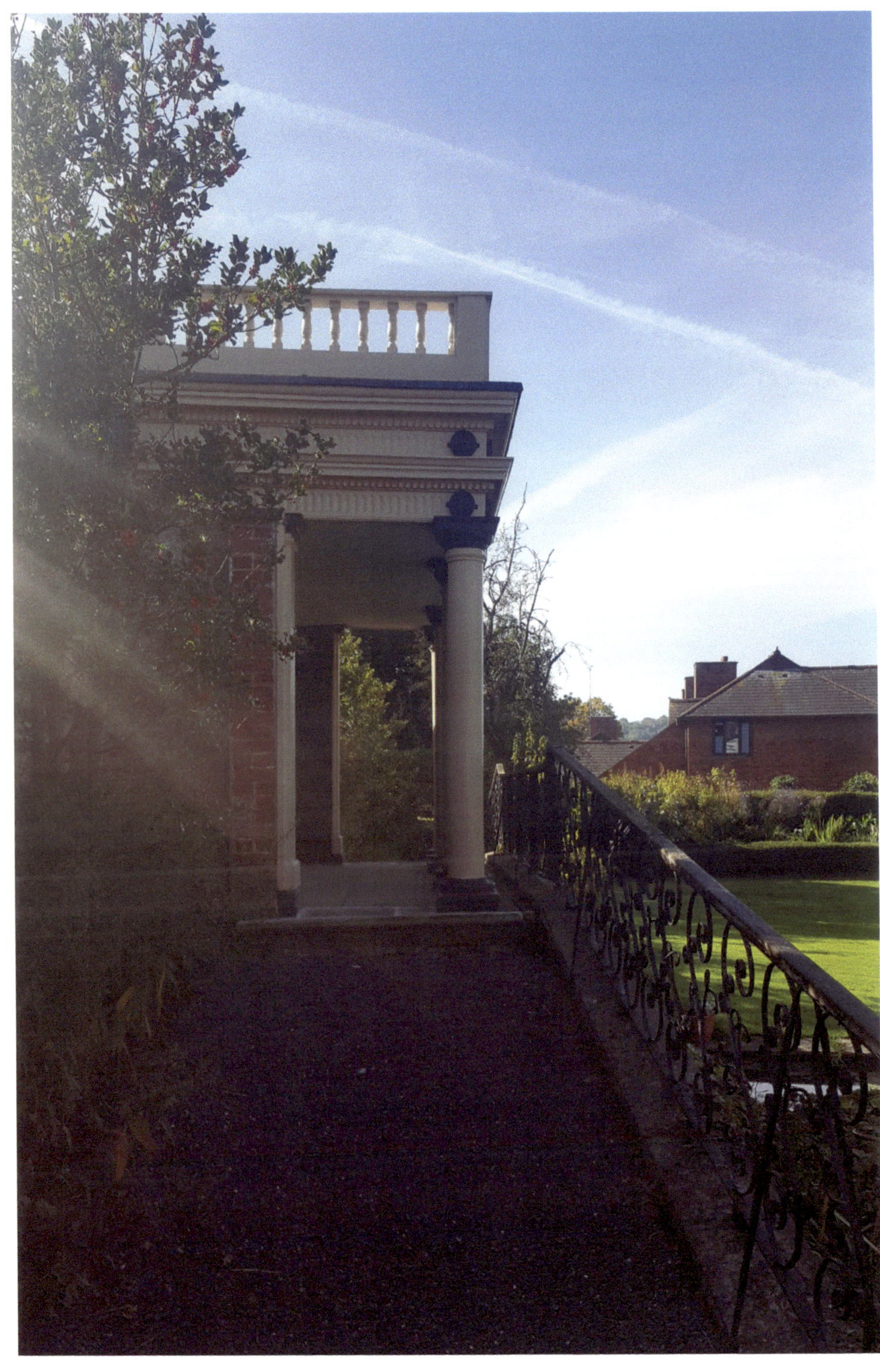

The 1840 pavilion.

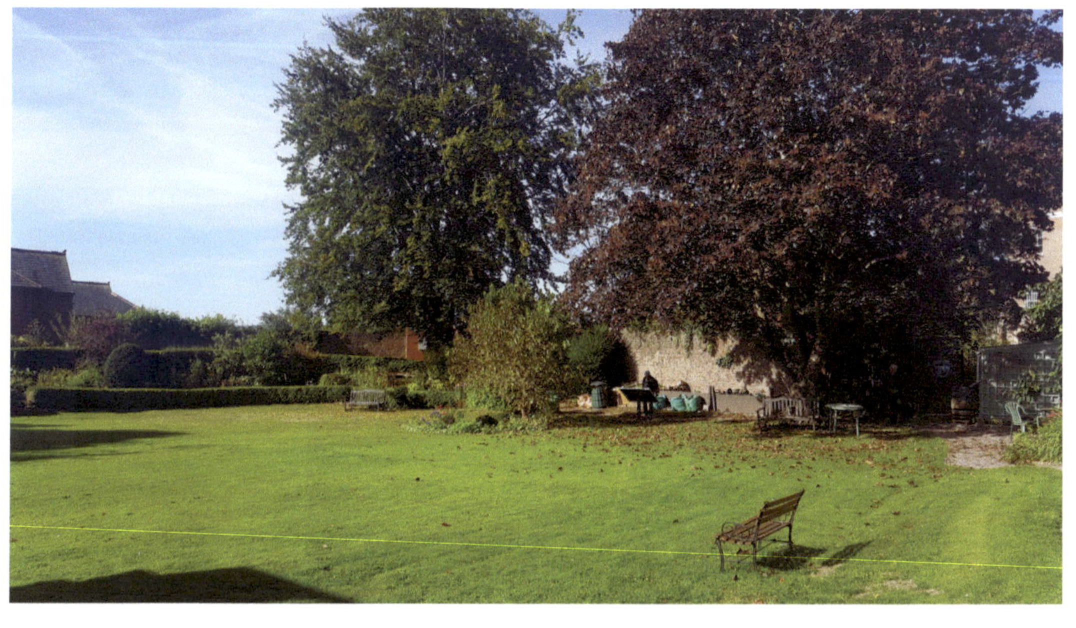

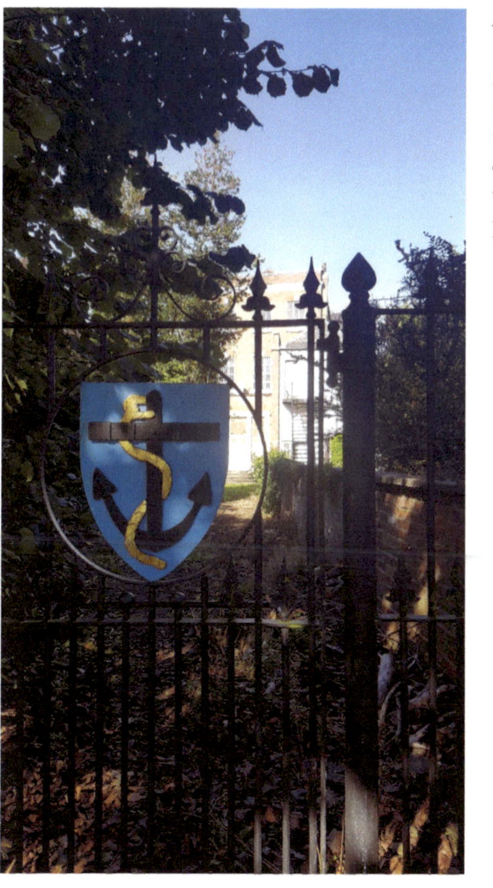

Above: View across the garden from the pavilion.

Left: Looking through from the Garden to the rear of Lloyds Bank, once a family home. There is a lost path that would have led from the house and to the right of the brick wall was the servants' 'alleyway', allowing unseen access from the house to the garden where produce was grown, as well as entertaining.

The north boundary wall of the garden is an eighteenth-century 'hot wall', which was heated by flues to ripen the fruit trees against it and prolong the growing season. Although popular in eighteenth-century kitchen gardens, not many survive but this one has survived in its entirety.

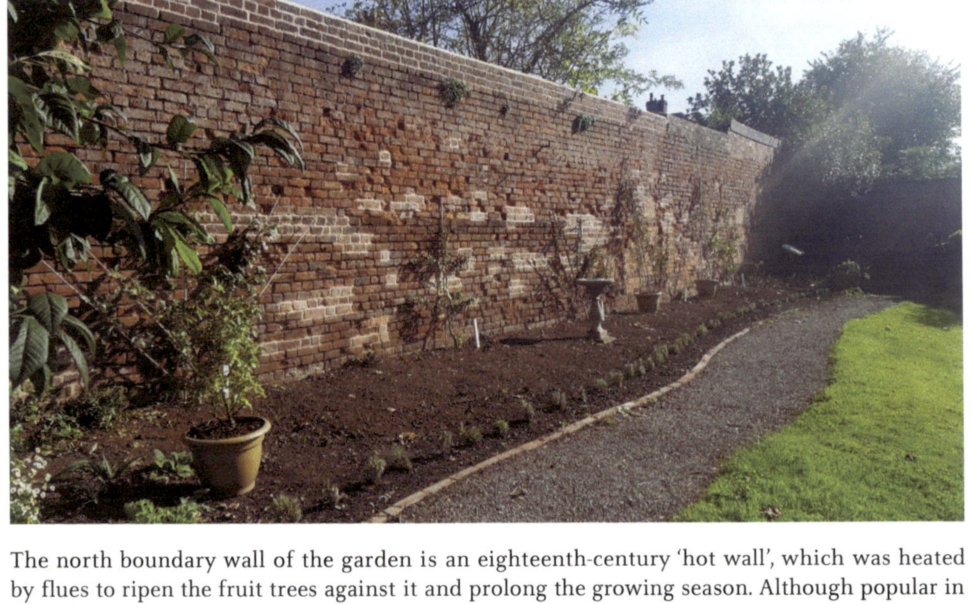

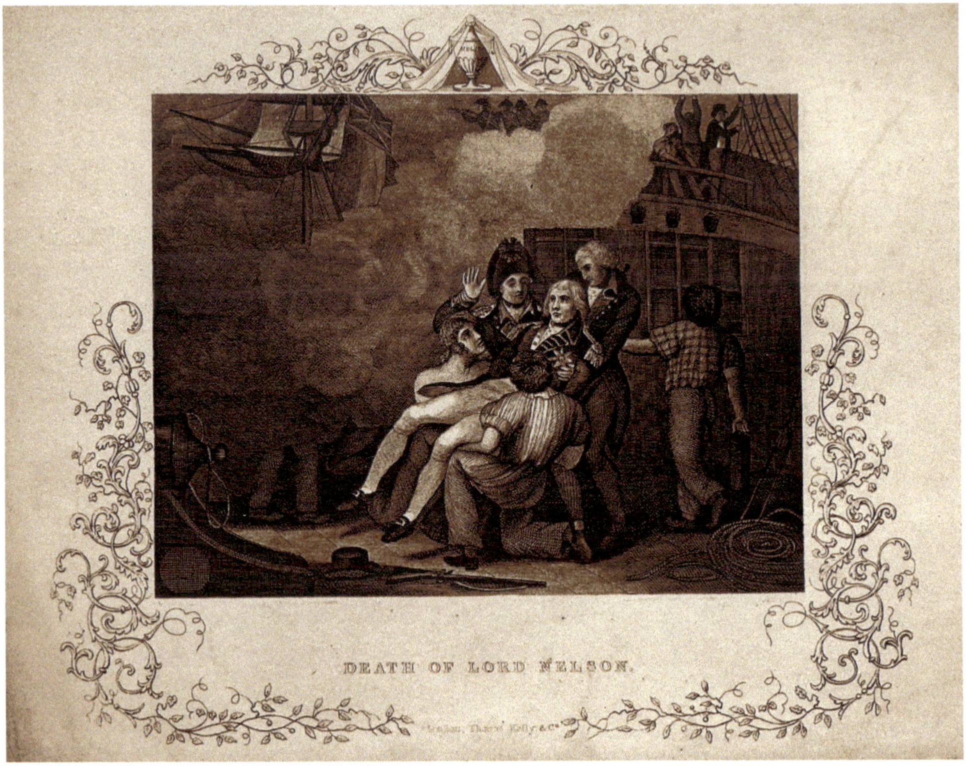

Three years after his Monmouth visit, Nelson was killed aboard his ship HMS *Victory* in the Battle of Waterloo, 1805. (Image courtesy of the Wellcome Library)

7. The Hendre Estate

The Hendre is situated approximately 5 miles north-west of the town of Monmouth. Hendre – meaning 'farm/homestead' in Welsh – did not come into the ownership of the Rolls family until 1767 when a cow keeper from London, John Rolls, married a wealthy heiress named Sarah Coysh, also from London. Sarah's mother was Rebecca Allen and her father was Thomas Coysh, and it was Rebecca's brother Henry Allen that lived at Hendre, then a hunting lodge/manor house. It was thanks to their ancestor James James (d. 1677), who owned farms and land in Monmouth and bought property in London between 1639 and 1648, that the family now had much wealth. The James family were namely in and around Southwark and Bermondsey areas, which were in the rural county of Surrey in James' day, and quite a way outside the original town of London.

Henry Allen died in 1767, bequeathing his Hendre estate to Sarah and her sister Elizabeth. Sarah outlived her sister, therefore becoming the sole heiress to the James, Allen and Coysh fortunes, which included land, farms and property in both London and Monmouth. It was the son of Sarah and John, known as John Rolls of the Hendre, that made Monmouth his family seat and began building and expanding of the manor house. This expansion continued over many years to the building we can see today, a Grade II listed Victorian mansion that remained in the Rolls family until 1984. It is now the home of the Rolls of Monmouth Golf Club. John Rolls of the Hendre was the great-grandfather of the most well-known member of the Rolls family, Charles Stewart Rolls.

DID YOU KNOW?
Charles Rolls was also an amateur musician and footballer, a keep-fit enthusiast who was also patron of a vegetarian restaurant.

Monmouth's famous son, Charles Stewart Rolls (1877–1910), born in Berkeley Square, London, was an avid engineer and aviator, son of the John Allen Rolls, 1st Baron Llangattock, politician and agriculturist, of the Hendre. His passion for cars began when, as an undergraduate at Cambridge in February 1896, he met Sir David Salomons, a scientific author, who had imported a car from France. By October 1896, Charles Rolls had himself imported a car and became of the earliest people in England to own one. In 1903, Charles Rolls started one of Britain's very first car dealerships in Fulham, London, with a financial handout from his father of £6,600 (approximately £500,000 in today's money). His friend, Henry Edmunds, was a director of a company in Manchester called

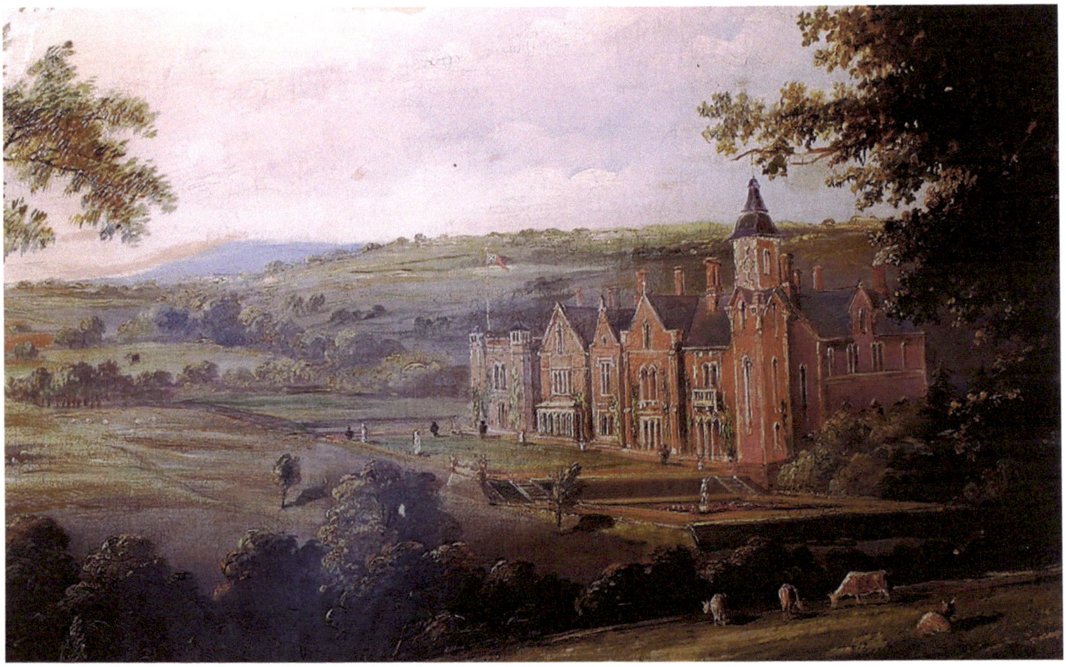

The Hendre, *c.* 1880s.

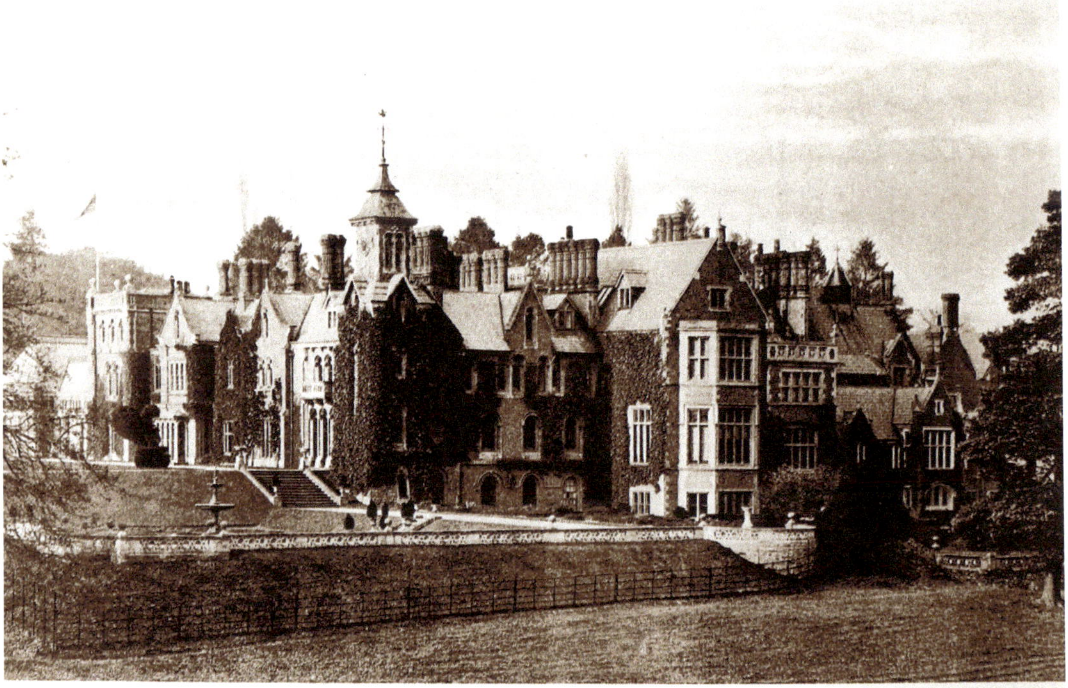

The Hendre, *c.* 1900.

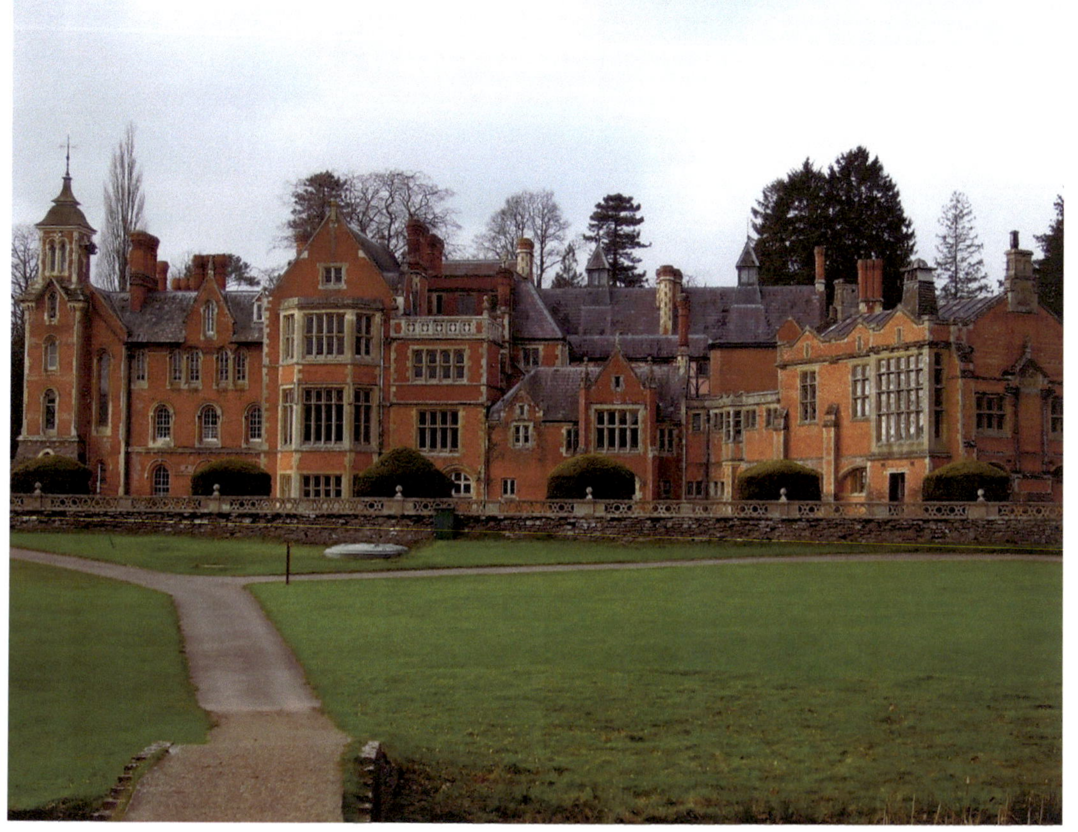

The Hendre, modern day. (Image courtesy of KJPI under Creative Commons 3.0)

Royce Ltd and in 1904, the co-founder of this company, Henry Royce, had designed and made his own car to his own high expectations after being disappointed in a car he had also imported from France.

Edmunds arranged the meeting between Henry Royce and Charles Rolls with a view to Royce selling his cars through Rolls' dealership while Rolls was looking for a high-quality manufacturer. Their business relationship had begun, although the company Rolls-Royce wasn't formed until 1906.

DID YOU KNOW?
Charles Rolls' first journey in his newly imported car was from London to Cambridge and he actually broke the speed limit. The Locomotive Act of 1878 restricted self-propelled vehicles to 4 mph and he had to have his car restricted and display a red flag.

Rolls had the glamour and the means to promote the Rolls-Royce engine, racing in America and breaking the record in the Monte Carlo to London race in a 20 hp Rolls-Royce. In September 1905, the first ever Tourist Trophy motor races were held on the Isle of Man; Rolls was the first entrant to go off the starter line but soon had the gears breakdown on him. This was thought to be sabotage as the same thing happened to another driver and they were both favourites to win. In 1906, however, Rolls won the races. Motorcycle races were held from 1907 and have been running every year, known as the Isle of Man TT Races.

A few years of adventure followed, including being one of the first people to fly with the Wright brothers in 1908 and importing one of the new 'aeroplanes' designed by Wilbur Wright to learn how to fly. In June 1910, Charles Rolls became a sensation after completing a non-stop, cross-channel return flight in a Wright plane but just two months later, at a flying tournament in Bournemouth, the tail end of his flying machine collapsed as he was landing, killing Charles Rolls.

Rolls had been the youngest of four children, with his eldest brother, John Maclean Rolls, being the 2nd Baron Llangattock. John died in 1916 from wounds sustained in the Battle of the Somme and his younger brother and heir presumptive, Henry Rolls, had died four months previous. Thus, the baroncy died with him and the family fortune, including Hendre and valued at £1.1 million (approximately £93 million today) passed to their sister Eleanor, who also died without issue. The inheritance then passed back to their aunt, Patricia Harding (née Rolls). Ergo, the surviving family became known as the Harding-Rolls.

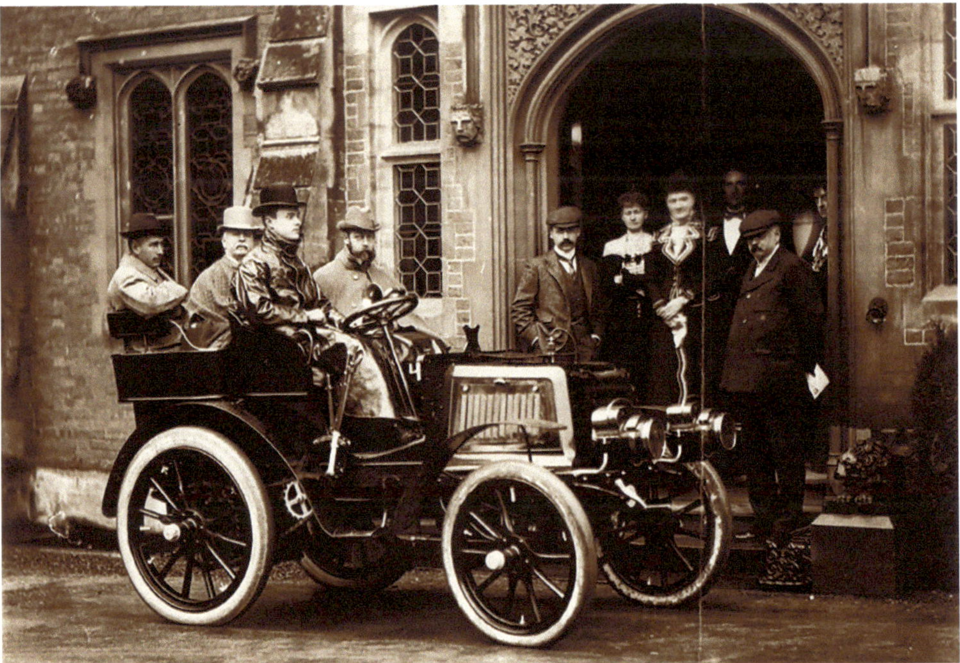

1900 at The Hendre. Charles Rolls (driving), who was around 6 feet 5 inches, with the Duke of York, the future king of England in the passenger seat; Lord Llangattock and Charles' father are on the right of the back seat next to the Duke of York's equerry. (Image courtesy of the National Archives)

DID YOU KNOW?
Eleanor Georgiana Rolls, sister of Charles, and the last baron, John McClean Rolls, married into the Shelley family of poet fame. She changed her name to Shelley-Rolls.

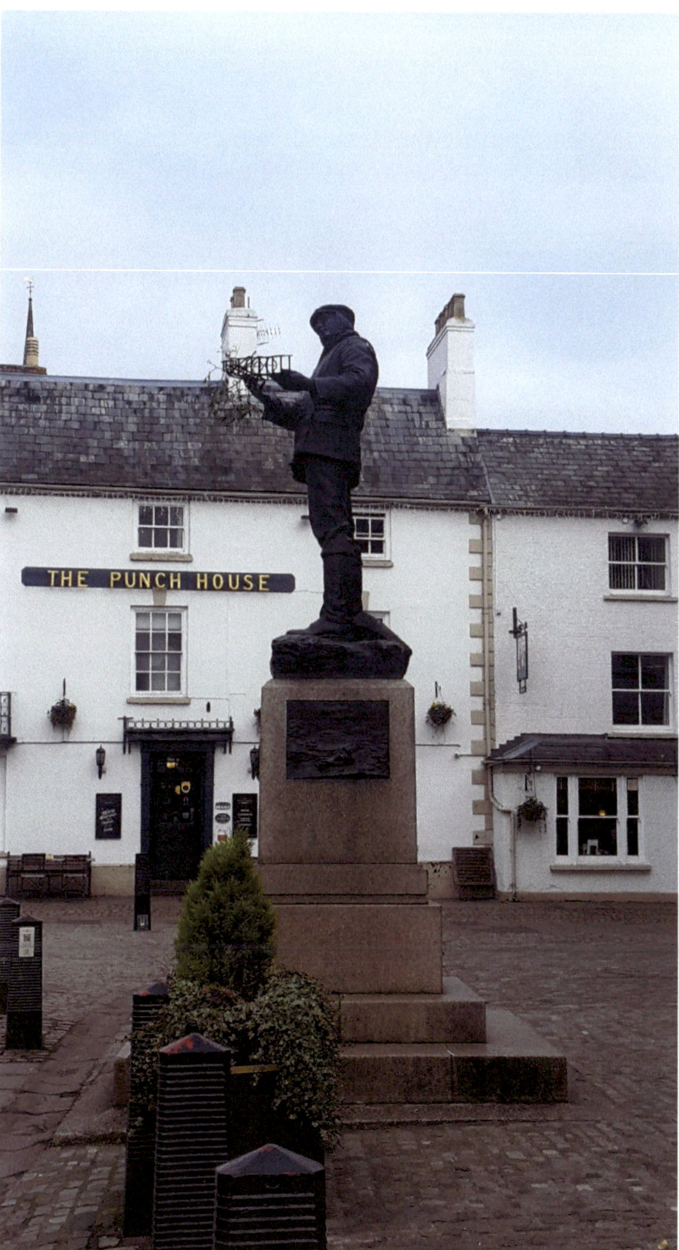

Statue of Charles Rolls outside the Shire Hall, Agincourt Square, Monmouth.

8. Historic Figures

Geoffrey of Monmouth

Researching Geoffrey within a limited time period was quite onerous as details around him are a tad vague. This section on him will go with an average of the sources available at the time, but his connection to Monmouth is without doubt.

Sources agree that Geoffrey was born in Monmouth between 1090 and 1100, and Geoffrey was also known as Galfridus Arturus, giving the impression his father may have been called Arthur. It was Geoffrey's monumental tome *Historia Regum Britanniae* (*History of the Kings of Britain*) that helped give rise to the legend of King Arthur, which grew in stature throughout the Middle Ages to the point it is hard to distinguish what was real and what was not. Geoffrey himself claimed he had translated documents from an ancient Welsh/British book, which has since been dismissed and based a lot on conjecture.

However, the Arthur part of his name may have been a scholarly nickname due to his flourished writings regarding King Arthur. He personally called himself Geoffrey of Monmouth, although he appears to have a weak grasp on the Welsh language at the time. It seems he was a Breton and, as mentioned in an earlier chapter, the Normans settled much wealth on Bretons who had supported their invasion of 1066. The Breton and Welsh (along with Cornish) languages were linguistically similar due to ancient trading and migration routes and Geoffrey's family may have had familial links with Gwethenoc, who founded Monmouth Priory.

DID YOU KNOW?
After John II of Monmouth handed Monmouth Castle back to the Crown, when Prince Edmund, 1st Earl of Lancaster and known as Crouchback, came into possession of the castle, he added the Great Hall. His grandson, Henry of Grosmont, 1st Duke of Lancaster, refurbished the upper floor of the Great Tower for comfort and was where Henry V was born.

Geoffrey had left Monmouth by the 1120s and spent most of his life in Oxford where he had access to manuscripts and writings lost to us now. While the majority of the *History of the Kings of Britain* has been regarded as fabrication and embellished by later historians, coupled with the workings of Geoffrey's over-imaginative mind, in today's world he would have been the historical novelist version of J. K. Rowling! Geoffrey's book had also spread throughout Western Europe. However, local historian David Hancocks writes there may be some grounding in Geoffrey's Arthurian legends. One of Geoffrey's sources was the Book of Llandaff, the Llandaff Charters, one of Wales's earliest ecclesiastical manuscripts, and while it may have been criticised over the years for being added to and complied for the purpose of a dispute, it appears that the Book of Llandaff had been validated by Pope Honorius II and many of the place/church names exist into modern day. Ergo, the Book of Llandaff can be considered an original source that mentions a king of Gwent called Arthur. However, whilst the Welsh Genealogies of the fifth and sixth centuries also mention Arthur, there is more than one named thus and the general consensus among scholars seems to be Arthur did indeed exist but was a warrior-general, not a king, revered by his people and of Romano-British descent. Geoffrey of Monmouth may have collected past ancient writings and put them altogether in around 1136, producing the *History of the British Kings* with his own spin, but many more after him have exaggerated and embellished, making it even more difficult to know if the possible warrior that was Arthur was based at Caerleon or Northumberland.

Geoffrey of Monmouth's patron was the powerful Robert, 1st Earl of Gloucester. Eldest illegitimate son of Henry I, his mother was probably from the Gay/Gayt family of Hampton and Northrook, Oxfordshire, where Henry I was known to have mistresses around his favourite castle of Woodstock. His father made Robert the 1st Earl of Gloucester

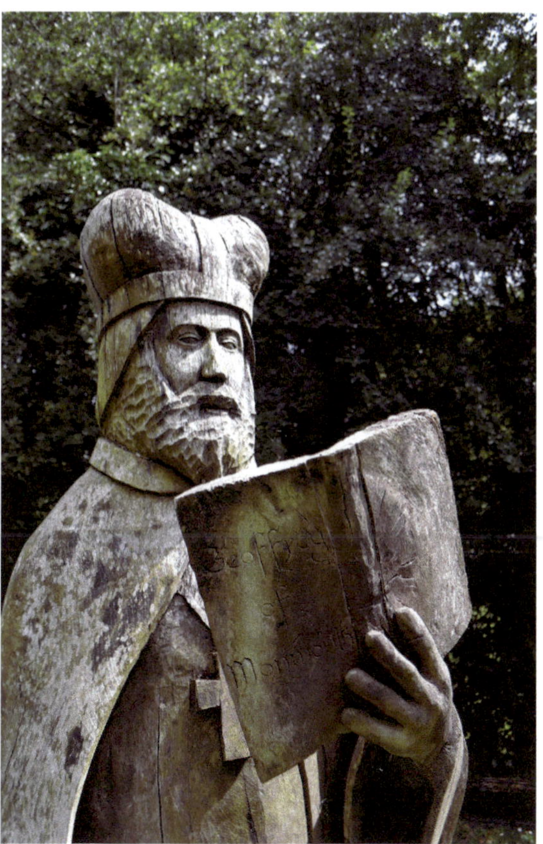

A wooden statue of Geoffrey of Monmouth at The Old Railway, Tintern. (Image courtesy of Colin Cheesman under Creative Commons 2.0)

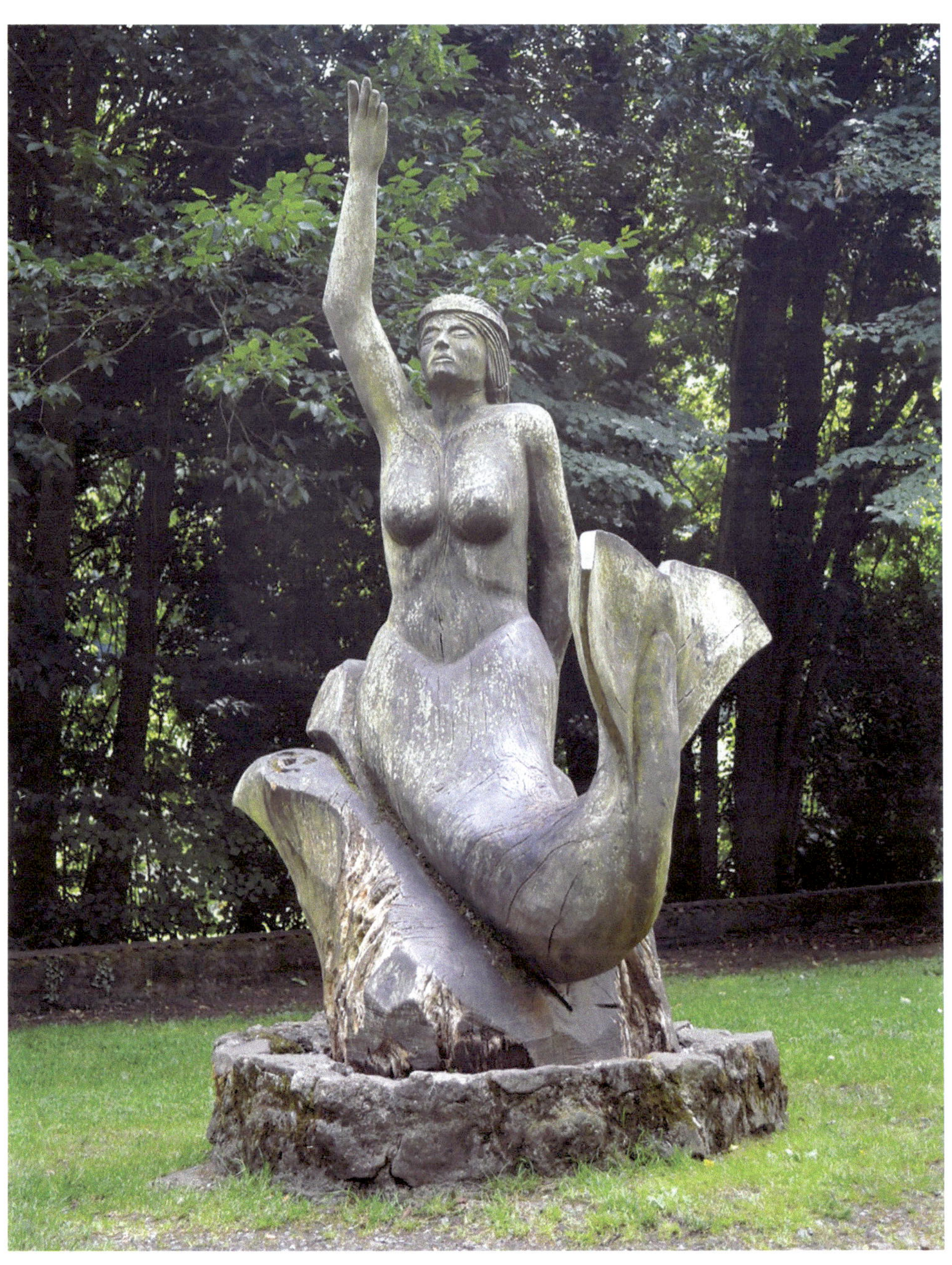

According to Geoffrey of Monmouth's *History of the Kings of Britain*, this is Sabren/Sabrina, Welsh name of Hafren/Habren, and goddess of the River Severn, so-called because she was the beautiful daughter of a king of the ancient Britons by his secret lover, a Germanic princess. The story goes that he divorced his queen, whom he had married for diplomatic reasons and also to keep peace with a king of Cornwall. He then married his lover, whom the ex-queen ordered to be thrown into the river along with her daughter, Hafren/Habren. The river was named after the daughter, morphing into Severn. However, etymological investigations show that while Severn is most probably a Romanized version of the Welsh Hafren/Habren, the origins are unknown. (Image courtesy of Colin Cheesman under Creative Commons 2.0)

A page from the *History of the Kings of Britain, c.* 1186. (Image courtesy of the British Library)

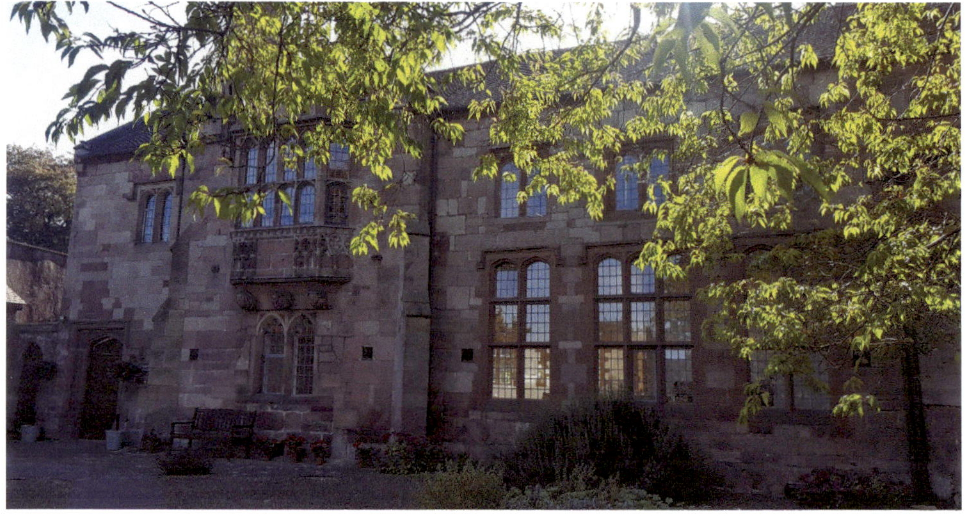

Facing Monmouth Priory from the gateway, with 'Geoffrey's Window' (top left oriel window) where he is thought to have written some of his work. He would have had the view over the Castle Field where the Battle of Monmouth would happen in 1233. Archaeology found here includes the remains of a high-status Roman building and also the largest undisturbed midden of twelfth-century pottery and bones. This was detritus from the kitchens of the monks that worked and lived in the same house at the same time as Geoffrey of Monmouth.

in 1121 and William of Malmesbury (England's foremost historian of the twelfth century and writing in the same era as Geoffrey of Monmouth) noted how Henry I relied heavily on the military judgement of his son, Robert. David Crouch, writing for the Oxford Dictionary of National Biography, describes Robert as:

one of the great aristocrats of his age. Between 1121 and his death he was rarely rivalled in England for power, wealth, and political influence. He was a consummate creature of the royal court, a great man of business, affable, and courtly. His consciousness of his own greatness comes through clearly in the work of his literary vassals, Geoffrey of Monmouth and William of Malmesbury: both tailor fulsome compliments to suit his taste, and address him as dux, not comes, equating his status with that of the great earls of pre-conquest England, or the continental dukes.

Geoffrey was made the Bishop of St Asaph in around 1152 but died in 1154/55. Sources differ as to where he died – some say Llandaff, others in London, while one source says unknown. One source gave his death at Flintshire, where his bishopric was, but other sources say Geoffrey never actually visited his bishopric due to the wars with Owain Gwynedd, so it appears to be bit of a mystery.

Henry V

Born in Monmouth Castle around August/September 1387, Henry of Monmouth (future Henry V) was the eldest son of Henry of Bolingbroke (future Henry IV) and his first wife

Mary de Bohun. Apparently, Monmouth Castle had been one of the favourite castles of his grandfather, John of Gaunt, son of Edward III, and John had entertained his mother, Queen Philippa, there in what became known as the Queen's Chamber. It was John of Gaunt's marriage to Blanche of Lancaster, daughter of 1st Duke of Lancaster, that bought Monmouth to Henry of Bolingbroke and thus was the birthplace of the future warrior king Henry V.

Mary Bohun was only around twelve years old when she was betrothed to Henry of Bolingbroke, fourteen when they married and after having a baby nearly every year following, she died in childbirth in 1394 aged approximately twenty-four. Henry of Monmouth was only seven when his mother died. He had spent his formative years at an isolated but safe country estate called Greenfield between Monmouth and Ross-on-Wye, renamed Courtfield in honour of him staying there, which is still the name it holds today under the Vaughan family – the current building was built in 1805 on the site of older buildings. He had uneventful childhood years, with evidence of Henry and his siblings spending time in the care of his maternal grandmother, Joan, Countess of Hereford, and sources agree there is not much documented on his childhood (he had not been born a royal prince so not a great deal of early information was recorded).

Some sources claim that Mary had a son four or five years older than Henry named Edward, born in 1382 but dying four days later and possibly buried in the Monmouth Castle Chapel. This would have made Mary only twelve/thirteen years old and it may have been mistaken that it was her nephew. Also, according to the castle and regimental museum, Henry V was born there as the family were on a tour of their estates – no mention of being on a tour when Mary would have been just twelve years old.

DID YOU KNOW?
The Minister's Accounts for Monmouth Castle in 1370 include items such as gallows for hanging robbers and the storage value of plague victims' goods. One of these was a Crowder (Crwth), a stringed musical instrument that is the origin of Monmouth family names such as Crowden, Crowther and Croudace.

There is a medieval wooden cradle that was allegedly that of the infant Henry V at Courtfield and became famous locally. In 1839 an antiquarian from Bristol procured the cradle for £30 (approximately £3,000 today) and by 1872 a William Watkins Old of Monmouth reported to the Royal Historical Society that the cradle and armour Henry V wore at Agincourt was stored at Troy House, the estate of the Beauforts. In 1908, the cradle was bought at a Christie's auction by Edward VII and it was kept at Windsor Castle until 1912 when Edward VII's successor, George V, donated the cradle to the new London Museum established at Kensington Palace. The solid oak cradle has since been proven to be of an age a century after Henry V but still a fine example of a medieval cradle.

Henry of Bolingbroke overthrew his cousin Richard II in 1399 to become Henry IV. Thus, aged thirteen, Henry of Monmouth became the Prince of Wales around the same

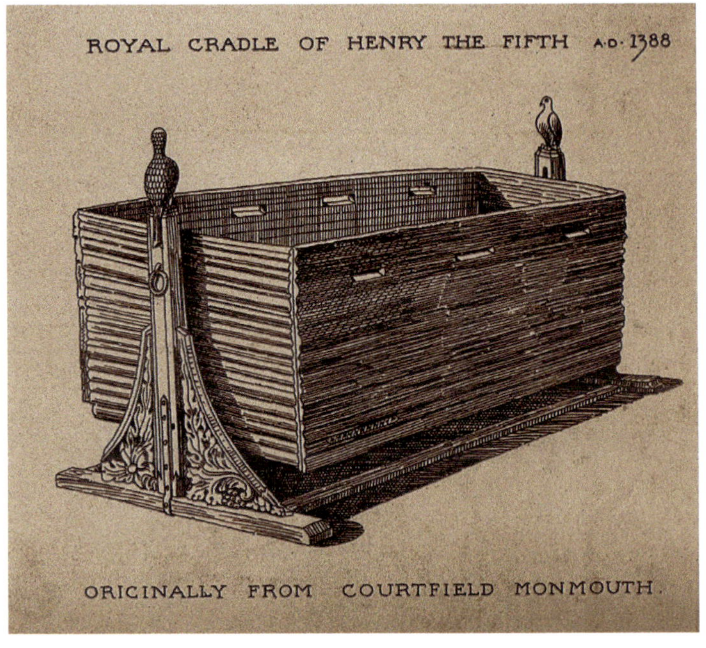

(Image courtesy of the Wellcome Collection)

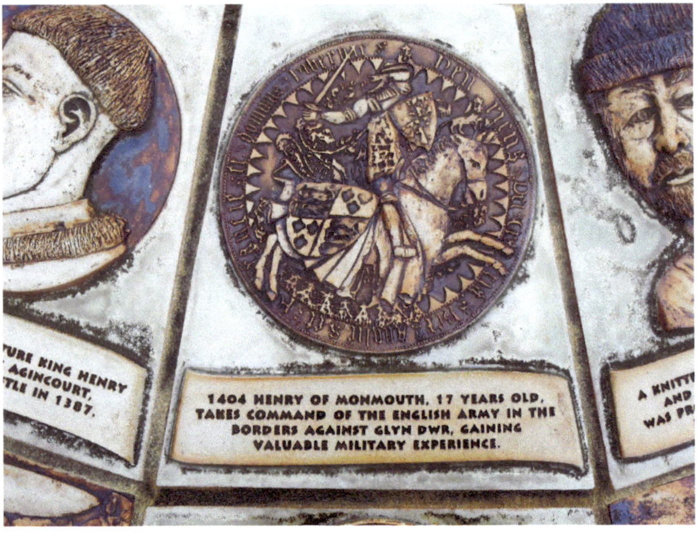

Henry V as Prince of Wales on the ceramic historical table by Monnow Bridge. (Image courtesy of Jambamkin under Creative Commons 3.0)

time that Owain Glyndŵr, the last Welsh Prince of Wales, instigated a war of independence against English rule in Wales. Initially, the Welsh revolt was a success against Henry IV but it was this conflict that gave Henry of Monmouth his first taste of warfare aged sixteen in the Battle of Shrewsbury 1403 against powerful foes. Free to utilise his own tactics, he proved himself a gifted tactician and fearless warrior. It is said that he used these tactics in fighting the French at Agincourt in 1415, the famous battle he became renowned for and which Agincourt Square is named after.

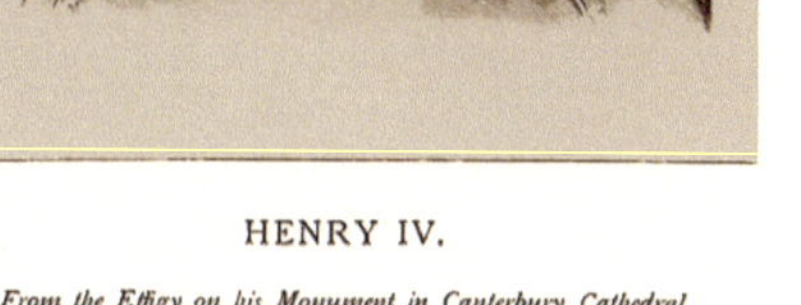

HENRY IV.

From the Effigy on his Monument in Canterbury Cathedral.

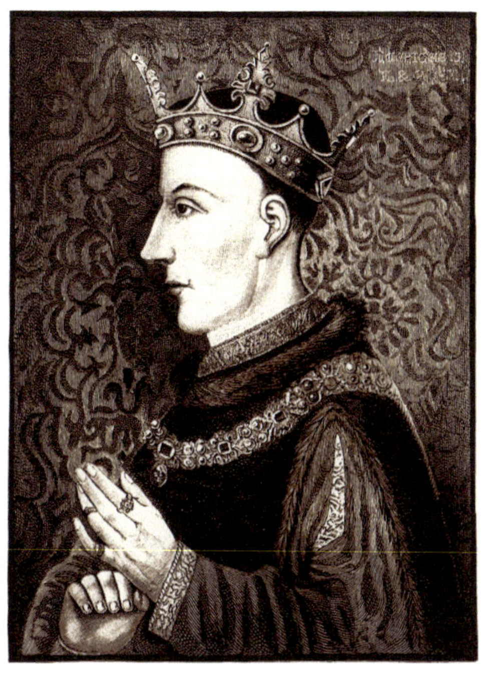

Above left: (Image courtesy of Hathi Trust)

Above right: A young Henry V, whose few portraits always show this side of his face after a severe wound obtained in the Battle of Shrewsbury when, aged sixteen, he had an arrow pierce the right side of his face just under the eye. The arrowhead was buried 6 inches into his head and was removed successfully by a battleground surgeon, who purposely made a tool to remove the arrow. This would have happened with no anaesthetic or antiseptic!

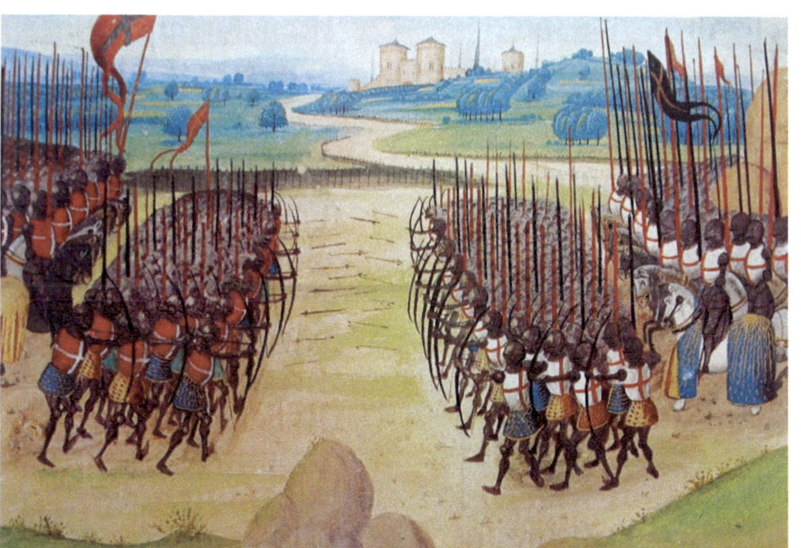

Battle of Agincourt, 1415, Henry V's great victory against an overwhelming French army.

Henry V died in 1422, still only around thirty-five years old. He probably died of dysentery (inflammation of the intestine caused by bacteria and resulting in diarrhoea, pain and fever; most often fatal in medieval times) after a siege in France.

Rockfield Studios

Amberley Court, a substantial farm/house on the B4322 out of Monmouth en route to the village of Rockfield, is mentioned in a will of Andrew Lewis, dated September 1746. In the early twentieth century it was the home and stables of horse breeders. The sixteenth-century Old Mill House was home for a time to the eccentric Major Sydney Herbert Charrington (1878–1954), a distinguished officer of the First World War. It was also prestigious fishing and country club in the 1950s. For the last thirty or so years, it has been a residential recording studio that doubles up as a bed and breakfast.

In 1963 the buildings were converted to a recording studio by two brothers, Charles and Kingsley Ward. Names like Queen, New Order, Manic Street Preachers, Simple Minds, Black Sabbath, Hawkwind and Dave Edmunds have stayed and recorded here. The Ward brothers went their own ways in the 1980s and on the Monnow Valley website it says:

Rockfield is still run by Kingsley but Monnow Valley has changed ownership a couple of times over the last few decades. In 2006, Monnow Valley was taken over by siblings Jo and James Hunt and has undergone substantial reinvestment since, including an acoustically engineered control room, new recording equipment, heating, air conditioning, redecoration and improved leisure facilities for the clients, making it one of the best recording studios in the UK. (www.monnowvalleystudio.com/history)

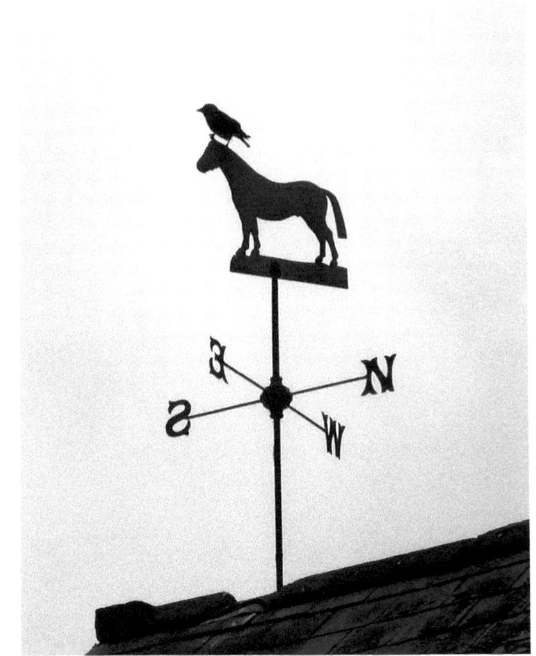

Purportedly the weathervane at Rockfield Studios, which inspired the last line of 'Bohemian Rhapsody' by Queen. 'Bohemian Rhapsody' was indeed recorded at Rockfield Studios in 1975. (Image courtesy of Siaron James under Creative Commons 2.0)

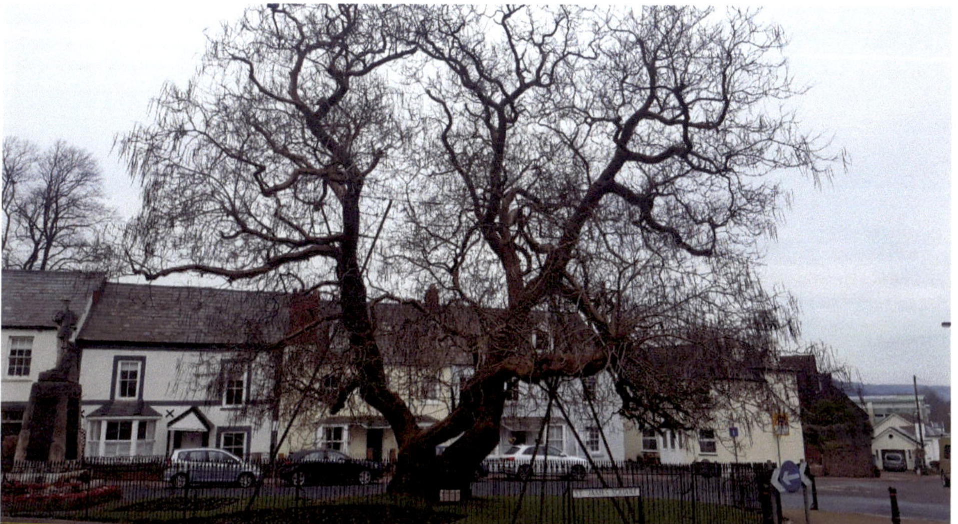

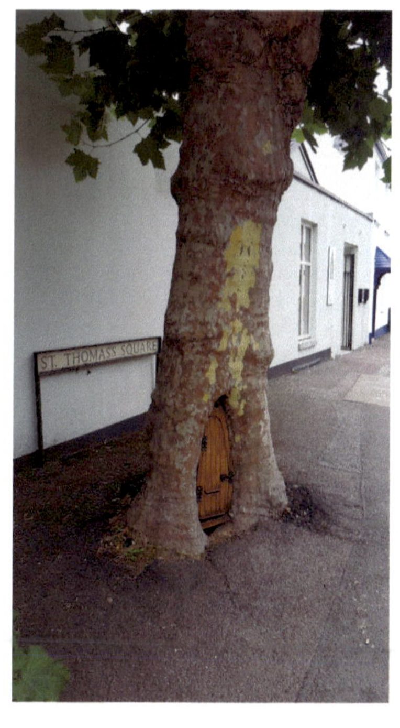

Above: The Indian Bean Tree in St James Square, planted in 1900 and thought to be one of the oldest and finest examples of its kind in the country. Despite the council wishing to cut it down and replant with a new bean tree in 2005, it was saved after some remedial work in 2006. The picture above is late 2018.

Left: The fairy tree in St Thomas's Square.

A Trim Shiere towne, for noble baron or knight,
A cittie sure, as free as is the best,
Where Size is kept, and learned lawyers rest,
Bright, Ancient, wise, in sweete and wholesome ayre
Where the best sort of people ofte repayre
Thomas Churchyard, 1587

Bibliography

Online sources
Wikipedia/media
www.britainexpress.com
www.british-history.ac.uk
www.CADW.gov.uk
www.castleswales.com
www.coflein.gov.uk
https://d.lib.rochester.edu/camelot/text/geoffrey [accessed 1.3.19]
www.gracesguide.co.uk
www.ggat.org.uk
www.gatehouse-gazetteer.info
www.haithitrust.org
www.historyextra.com
www.monasticwales.org
www.monmouthshire.gov.uk
www.monnowvalleystudio.co.uk [accessed 19.2.19]
www.monrem.com
www.newpapers.library.wales
http://www.newworldencyclopedia.org/entry/Ammianus_Marcellinus [accessed 2.2.19]
www.opendomesday.org.uk
www.ordancesurvey.co.uk [accessed 29.1.19]
www.overlookingthewye.org.uk
https://www.rct.uk/collection/72098/cradle-and-stand [accessed 19.2.19]
www.roadsofromanbritain.org
www.specialcollections.le.ac.uk
www.thegazette.co.uk/London/issue/14019/page/559/data.pdf [accessed 1.2.19]
www.therollsgolfclub.co.uk/history [accessed 29.12.18]
https://www.telegraph.co.uk/news/obituaries/law-obituaries/5090475/Earl-Nelson.html
https://www.forestofdeanhistory.org.uk/assets/PDF/Newsletters/Downloadable-
    NEWSLETTER-May-2016.pdf [accessed 1.2.19]
www.visionofbritain.org.uk
www.welcometomonmouth.co.uk [accessed 3.3.19]
www.workhouse.co.uk [accessed 1.3.19]

Books
Anglo-Saxon Chronicle (James Ingram translation).
Benedictow, Ole J., *The Black Death 1346–1353: The Complete History* (Boydell Press, 2018).

Brady, L, *Writing the Welsh Borderlands in Anglo-Saxon England* (Manchester University Press, 2017).

Buckland, K. *The Monmouth Cap* (1979). Available from www.renactor.ru [accessed 1.2.19].

Burton, J., Stöber, K., *Abbeys and Priories of Medieval Wales* (University of Wales Press, 2015).

Clarke, S., 'Down the Dig: Monmouth, An Adventure in Archaeolog' (Monmouth Archaeological Society, 2008).

Coates, S.D., *The Water Powered Industries of the Lower Wye Valley* (1992).

Coxe, W., *An Historical Tour in Monmouthshire* (1801) Available from https://babel. hathitrust.org/cgi/pt?id=gri.ark:/13960/t72v5dm2v;view=1up;seq=9

Davies, J., *A History of Wales* (Penguin, 2007).

Eden, S. F. M., *State of the Poor* (London, 1797).

Faletra, Michael, *Geoffrey of Monmouth's The History of the British Kings* (Broadview Press, 2007).

Hancocks, *David King Arthur and the Monnow Valley* (Valley Publishing, 2013).

Heath, C., The Historical and Descriptive Accounts of the Ancient and Present State of the Town of Monmouth (Charles Heath, 1804).

Hindle, Paul, *Medieval Roads and Tracks*, 3rd ed. (Shire Archaeology, 2016).

Higham, N., *King Arthur* in the Pocket Giants series (The History Press, 2015).

Kinross, J., *Castles of the Marches* (Amberley, 2015).

Kissack, K., *Medieval Monmouth* (The Monmouth Historical and Educational Trust, 1975).

Kissack, K., *Monmouth: the Making of a County Town* (Phillimore, 1975).

Kissack, K., *The River Severn* (Lavenham Press, 1982).

Kissack, K., *The River Wye* (Lavenham Press, 1978).

Oxford Dictionary of National Biography.

Ramsay, *Sir James Henry, Lancaster and York: a Century of English History* (1399–1485) (Oxford, 1892).

Records of Bristol Ships 1800–1838 (Vessels over 150 tons) Vol. XV (1950).

Roberts, D., *The Story of Drybridge House and the Crompton-Roberts Family* (2004).

Roderick, A., *Unknown Gwent* (Village Publishing, 1986).

Rowlands, M. J., *Monnow Bridge and Gate* (Alan Sutton Publishing, 1994).

Sivier, D., *Anglo-Saxon and Norman Bristol* (Tempus, 2002).

Tolstoy, C., *The Mysteries of Stonehenge: Myth and Ritual at the Sacred Centre* (Amberley, 2016).

Waugh, R. *The Illustrated Handbook to Monmouth* (Oxford University, 1875).

Weir, A., *Britain's Royal Families: the Complete Genealogy* (Vintage, 2008).

Winn, C., *I Never Knew That About Wales* (Random House, 2007).

Wright, T., *The Wanderings of an Antiquary* (Nicholas & Sons, 1854).

Wyatt, L., *Secret Chepstow* (Amberley, 2018).

Wyatt, L., *Secret Hayes* (Amberley 2018).